Practice Learning

Perspectives on globalisation,
citizenship and cultural change

Practice Learning
Perspectives on globalisation, citizenship and cultural change

edited by

Graham Ixer

Whiting & Birch Ltd
MCMVI

Published by Whiting & Birch Ltd,, London SE23 3HZ, England.
ISBN 1 86177 051 0
Printed in England and the United States byLightening Source

Contents

Foreword

I am delighted to write the foreword for this book, the first in a series to be published in association with the *Journal of Practice Teaching in Health and Social Work*. Globalisation is a relevant and important subject for all those engaged in the education process for health and social care. Graham Ixer has worked with presenters at the Third International Conference to produce a book that will enhance the understandings of students, practitioners and educators within the field. This book is a valuable contribution to our understanding of the differences in practice and polemic around the world. We should all strive to move from a Eurocentric vision of health and social care in order to inform our practice. International agreement of what is social work is an agenda we should all strive to work towards. Given the inherent tensions within this paradigm, this book is a useful tool which will help us identify the areas of agreement and difference within an International context. I know that I have enjoyed reading it and have found it an interesting and important contribution to our growing understanding of the context within which health and social care work is delivered around the world.

Lynda Deacon
Founding and Managing Editor.

Introduction

Graham Ixer

The majority of this book is a series of essays presented at the 3rd international conference – 'Values, Culture and Ethics: The Changing Face of Practice Learning' for the Journal of Practice Teaching in Health and Social Work, at York England, in April 2004. Because of the expanding debate on practice learning and the need to understand globalisation and its impact on professional learning, the journal has collected a wide range of critical essays that present different perspectives from around the world. The main theme of this book is the effects globalisation has on practice learning for those social workers and health workers in training. Far to often social workers and nurses train in isolation with little knowledge of what is happening in their own profession let alone from a broader international perspective. The book takes different themes on practice learning and examines them in the context of globalisation, citizenship and cultural change. The different perspectives are drawn from research and practice experiences from a diverse range of continents: Africa, Asia, North and South America, Australia and Europe.

As UK social workers, nurses or allied health workers start their training and learn their trade by practising in the field, what they learn in college is carried out in practice within a localised context. Whether the practicum be a social services office, a NHS hospital or primary care facility the focus is often an anglicised, eurocentric view of care, or as Dixon and Pearce describe as the 'Anglo-Social welfare state' (2005. p.62). It may be argued that this is reasonable given that such practitioners will generally be regionally located when they qualify and practise.

However, I would argue that professionals in training require a much wider perspective and experience in their training. The need to expose themselves to greater critical and international debate in areas such as culture, globalisation, political economy, democracy and citizenship and is crucial if we want to achieve well informed, able practitioners. However, some would counter this argument by saying social policy is already an integral part of their curriculum (Parker and Bradley, 2003, quoted in Doel and Shardlow, 2005, p.87). I would question how much practitioners are consciously aware of the global issues affecting their core business of social work? Social services and the NHS health system are social structures of care. Yeates (2005) argues that such social structures

> require us to reflect on how people and institutions are entangled in trans-territorial processes and attend to the connections between global, national and sub-national spheres. (p.232)

In this context social work operates *'on the front line of 'social exclusion' and citizenship'* (Rimmer, 2005). Rimmer goes onto say that *'full citizenship and inclusion will only be achieved when excluded people have their say in the democratic process'* (p.2). Yet as will be seen in some of the follow chapters in this book, inclusion and citizenship are complex ideas that are not easily achievable in a democratic society operating in a global context of terrorism, economic instability and commercial uncertainty.

This book presents a series of global perspectives on practice learning with the intention of critically debating the comfort zone that many professionals place themselves in and often resist from changing. The new millennium has brought about considerable change and more importantly a very different world. Besthorn and McMillen in describing the aftermath of the 'Twin Towers' disaster in New York, talk about the need to face up to ever growing social problems that are more a consequence of economic, political and social failure then personal failure. Globalisation and consumer driven 'marketisation' are

> creating international systemic problems which are producing new forms of oppression and are escalating poverty, environmental decline and physical and mental illness on a global scale. (2002, p.29).

They argue that challenging this should be the future project of all social workers.

The serious affect of such consumerism on the most vulnerable and displaced in our society is enormous and one which social workers, nurses and other professionals need to counter with relentless energy, commitment and political aptness. By working closely to their core professional values social workers and health professionals will find a way through the complexity of challenges made on their ethical practice. As can be seen in the chapters in this book, social care and health professionals across the globe share similar values despite their location in different institutions, social structures and competing political, economic and ideological divergence.

Despite such divergence, Sewpaul and Jones (2004) argue for the bring together of international social work through global standards, an ideal that many would support but few are able to realise in practice. Although they identify what social work is as a basis to which standards are formed, international agreement of this is still far apart. In many countries social work is an activity described differently as can be seen in the first chapter in Mead and Wild's work on community health care. Gray and Fook also argue similarly to Mead and colleagues and draw a distinction between 'international social work' and 'universal social work' (2004, p.625). The debate on what is social work is not helped by a lack of international comparative studies on (Nagy & Falk, 2000).

Despite world changes driven by globalisation professions such as social work have to fight their corner in protecting it as a discrete profession in its own right in the same way nurses and doctors themselves have successfully achieved over many years. Professional regulation in the UK has helped to cement the professional identity of social work in the UK through codes of practice (GSCC, 2003) and the legal protection of title of 'social worker' (HMSO, 2000).

Globalisation affects social work in many ways, therefore it is reasonable to assume it will affect the practice that supports students' learning. Examples of this can be found in many ways across the globe with economic markets changing, creating large scale migration of traditional labour markets and consequently, different social problems resulting in community dysfunction. Although not everyone shares this view of how globalisation has affected the world, some see as leading to myths rather than realities – *'the impact of these processes of economic globalisation and regionalisation has been less extensive than originally feared'* (Dixon and Pearce, 2005, p.63).

This book is a polemic on these and other related issues and the tensions that exist for professionals learning in practice from different parts of the world. The intention is not only to inform debate but also develop it further so professionals training in practice are able to engage more politically, challenge more appropriately, take better informed risks and utilise their energy more creatively for the benefit of users of health and social care. In doing this we strengthen the role of the professional from moving away from a self-protected interest to a more open, engaging accountable profession.

However, other problems face professionals. Besthorn in a recent keynote presentation (2005) gave a powerful argument of 'hidden forces at work' in North America that serve to restrict rather than liberate social work practice. Due to world terrorism the US government introduced what is known as the 'Patriot Act' which gave it unprecedented powers to intervene in peoples' lives, use under-cover surveillance and detain without charging anyone believed to be a terrorist. Social workers are being required to hand over detailed case notes and reveal personal information on their clients of whom many are foreign nationals. This challenges the social worker's core values and code of practice. It breaches the confidentiality built up in their relationship with the service user. The issue here is not whether morally the government is right or wrong, in unusual times one has to take unusual action, but more important for the issues relevant to this book, how national and international policy directly affect local practice. Professionals must look beyond their own territory, understand the wider international picture of social change, the drivers of such change and the globalised effects on social welfare. Rather than passively play the recipients of change, one needs to be the force for change, open debate and influence others. Social workers and health professionals need courage to face up to their problems (Thompson 2005:185), but moreover a commitment to challenge their own institutions let alone their government who in some countries regularly and openly oppress those people with whom they intend to serve and are in most need of help. Yet in some countries such as Israel, Sudan, Iraq, Iran, Afghanistan, and Turkey community health workers and social workers are very used to working with oppressive regimes yet still find creative ways of supporting their clients in difficult circumstances. This is explored in more detail in some of the following chapters and shows how practice learning across the world is different with different challenges, opportunities and issues that are drawn together under one theme, that is the world is now a smaller place. This brings about positive opportunities for sharing and learning together, yet conversely, problems of global terrorism and economic turbulence in a new 21st century. As modern practitioners we must become more aware of how these changes affect us so we can counter the affect this has on service users who so often become the passive pawns in a much larger game.

* * *

In Chapter 1, Wild and Meads looks at practice teaching in a global world. The context for health and social care as a result of post-millennium modernisation is significant change. They examine the concept of modernisation and its impact on changing policy, regulation, governance and inter-professional relationships and as a result, the emerging new environment for practice learning. Through wide spread international research in primary health care they highlight important developments in interprofessional education and a framework for collaboration in future practice learning. Some of their most significant developments come from the most unusual places, for example, in developing countries in Africa where so called 'developed countries' have much to learn in health and social care.

In Chapter 2, McCafferty undertakes a comparison study on practice learning from his own social work programme, Partnership Care West in Northern Ireland and a new model developed at Haifa University in Israel. The focus draws on the outcomes of group supervision in practice learning and their exposure to globalised learning from other cultures. The Northern Ireland partnership programme is immersed in economic, political, historical and cultural tradition which characterises its approach to social work training. McCaffety argues the importance of opening up their programme to wider global learning. Using the findings from Haifa university demonstrates how social workers in training need wider exposure to globalised trends and influences to understand the full impact of globalisation on social work practice. It is only by doing this will social workers develop international perspectives and make a significant contribution to a new emerging discourse on international practice learning.

In Chapter 3, Muleya examines African culture and its impact on practice learning for social work students. For those practice educators whose tradition and cultural training originates outside of Africa lack insight into the effect and benefit of African cultural learning. Such understanding can benefit the learning environment of the student and offer an alternative paradigm to the western socio-political and eurocentric tradition in professional education. Many African social workers train in the UK yet the dominant learning paradigm excludes the background tradition for African black culture and what it might offer social work in the west. Using ecological and systems theory, Muleya argues how influential patterns of socialisation within African culture can positively benefit professional learning of African students in the UK. More critically Muleya tackles the difficult concept of What is culture to contextualised a framework for understand diversity and difference in professional education? In a changing political environment that grounds social work in Western methodology this essay is a refreshing exposure to an alternative dimension in professional training.

In Chapter 4, Ambler and Black report on their experience training social work practice educators in the Chernihiv law College in northern Ukraine. The purpose of the visit was to examine where the UK values critical to UK social work training are able to transfer to other cultures. During a first visit in 2000 they taught a five-day module on practice learning and used research tools of questionnaire, structural interviews and focus groups to collate and analyse data that sought to examine the transferability of values. Practice teachers have no formal training. The effects of their teaching and transferability of knowledge and values are evident in the positive changes to practice teaching brought about because of their visit.

In Chapter 5, Miller looks at practice learning from a feminist North American perspective and how the cultural and historical tradition of training in North America has influenced social work practice. Drawn from her own experience as a social worker, Miller cleverly traces the historical roots of social oppression and its impact on national and global policy change in north American social work. The idea of cultural competence and social diversity are two key concepts underpinning her main discourse on practice learning and are explored in some depth. Miller concludes with several challenges, in particular, to bridge the gap between theory and practice and to counter culture constraints with incorporating 'compassion' into everything we do. Her ideas for realising a vision for cultural competence are shared in persuasive language.

In Chapter 6, Weber examines what is sensitive cultural practice in Australia. She considers her own practice and its fit with received wisdom from codes of practice for social workers in first world countries. The focus of the chapter is about building respect for diversity and difference in practice learning so learners can benefit from studying alongside people from different cultural backgrounds. She argues how post-modern influences and critical questioning are seen to inform cultural sensitivity and ethical practice. Working to professional codes, one's own ethical practice and the difference in culture of those recipients of social work offer individual intellectual challenges to social work students and the legitimacy of developing a multi-perspective understanding of difference and cultural diversity. This chapter offers insight and alternative ways of understanding the cultural phenomenon of ethical practice.

In Chapter 7, Mak takes a Hong Kong Chinese perspective on social work training. She examines the Hong Kong tradition in social work education and the impact of globalisation. This is followed by an analysis of traditional Chinese culture from the cultural imperative to themes taken from the Confucian tradition. The importance of 'indigenisation' of social work in Hong Kong is explored to show the journey of travel that has taken place. Finally Mak presents how these changes and predicted new changes impact on practice learning and offer an alternative paradigm on practice learning.

In my own chapter 8 an analysis of the prevailing, political agenda of service user involvement is examined. This is viewed in the context of dong one's civic duty in providing universal public services. The UK experience is briefly examined in the context of international comparisons. Professional training in social work has seen a significant development in the involvement of social care service users in the planning, delivery and evaluation of training. UK governments have given greater significance to the involvement of service users in the delivery of care. In health, patients and public are incorporated into new policies and institutions bring them to the forefront of better health care. These developments are explored in this essay tracking the historical roots of citizenship and the relationship between public duty and public involvement. Practice learning in the UK manifests a core principle of service user involvement and empowerment yet the discourse of service user involvement takes place in isolation to the debate on civic involvement. This chapter concludes with an argument that both these discourses are relational but are not being debated by social workers in training, therefore creating misunderstanding and an emerging intellectual and social ignorance on the aetiology of an emerging discourse in service user involvement.

In Chapter 9 Hume looks at the complex process of communication in the interview context. She analyses cultural communication in the way people use non-verbal language, emphasis, metaphor and silence. These communicative dimensions provide support for effective communication but also barriers that if not read correctly, result in poor or miscommunication. Hume explores this area and offers a new tool for analysing communicative inquiry. This chapter provides insight into how cultural linguistics can be understood from an Australian perspective but also its wider applicability across global continents. It is argued that there is a commonality in communication provided by the 'Hume Inquiry Tool' that offers a broader application to communication in teaching and counselling across the world.

In the final Chapter Besthorn gives a critical polemic on the effects of globalisation on society, and ultimately social work practice and therefore, social work practice learning. This brings together the political context for the entire book. He argues that the drive towards greater materialism and economic consumerism is at a price for dismantling individual and community responsibility towards ethical practice. In his analysis of global capitalism he reflects on the very essence of social welfare and social work as activators of social reform and change. Yet the paradox caused by global capitalism is that society acts against social reform and social justice as a necessary evil to bring about materialistic prosperity. This is in opposition to the very purpose of social work. The ideological stance of consumerism is balanced against the ethical practice of social redistribution. These concepts are complex but Besthorn argues a new way of knowing and therefore a new way of learning in practice. Besthorn ends with re-defining the need for a new and more ethical social work project that extends beyond westernised ideology and takes us across the globe - social work requires a new vision of globalisation, revised definition of social justice, and new and more creative ways to enhance the capacity of all people in all societies.

This book is relevant for social worker and health professionals who are either students, practitioners, managers or policy planners because we all have a crucial role to play in preparing students to become competent practitioners. Barnett eloquently epitomises what the task is for professionals in training.

> We have to recognise that educating for professional competence can never be a matter of supplying students with predefined skills and knowledge to be turned on to situations. Professional action at the highest level, is unpredictable and presents situations of such complexity that no straightforward solutions may be available in predetermined outcomes. (Barnett, 1992, p.189)

Social work is a globalised industry with uncertainty and unpredictability in way that we have never experienced before, for this reason we have to think differently about the scope and nature of learning so students can be exposed to the widest range of creative and positive learning opportunities in practice. We owe it to our future practitioners that they learn as much as they can from our colleagues around the world. We must bury our terrortorialism and open our boundaries of inclusivity to ensure all practice curricula includes an international dimension so we are better prepared to cope with the changes confronting our profession.

1

Practice teaching in a global world

Andrea Wild and Geoffrey Meads

Introduction: Context and approach

As a result of post-Millennium 'Modernisation' the context for health and social care practice is fundamentally changing. The term 'Modernisation' signifies an international pattern of policies for decentralisation, regulation, governance, innovative partnerships and national stewardship of social capital which taken together create a new environment for the local teaching of this practice. Overall the contemporary environment is characterised by a shift from individual profession to host organisation as principal locus of care, while at the same time the boundaries of health and social care organisational units have themselves become less fixed and more flexible. Alliances, cooperatives, networks and other forms of joint ventures abound as part of the general movement away from simple institutional or market models to complex systems based approaches rooted in relationships. For practice teaching collaboration in this context becomes both the educational process and the educational objective or outcome. Essential requirements for membership of a modern health and social care profession are interprofessional skills and competencies.

An awareness of this changing context led the UK Department of Health and London based Health Foundation in 2002 to commission a long term programme of research designed to promote 'transferable learning' between countries with parallel 'modernising' policy reforms in health and social care (Wild et al, 2003). There was a particular UK interest, given the recent introduction across England of Primary Care Trusts with their multiprofessional management mechanisms, in novel community based organisational practices (Meads et al, 2005a). Different approaches to both interprofessional learning and development and combining health and social services were defined as priority subjects for transferable learning. This chapter draws on some of the lessons that have emerged from this research programme, the detailed methodology of which has been reported elsewhere (Meads et al, 2005b). The aim of the chapter is twofold: first to highlight both collective and individual developments in interprofessional education (IPE) that can positively inform present practice; and secondly to offer a framework of collaboration for its future teaching.

On both counts there are new challenges and opportunities. The opportunities are especially apparent in practice teaching for social care given its longer history of service development across the statutory and non-statutory sectors. Health care education has historically been more unidisciplinary with less emphasis in curricula design on, for example, community development, teamwork, participation and networking. For social care practitioners working with voluntary agencies, 'substitute' professionals and private enterprise partners has become standard practice and such learning is a pragmatic necessity. The tenets of modernisation now mean the same for their health care counterparts. With decentralisation, for example, come local resource management arrangements cutting across professions and communities. These range from the hybrid Primary Health Organisations of New Zealand that cluster the community based professionals of private general practices into unified public health programmes, to the various skill mixes tendered for by Thailand's Contracting Units for Primary Care (Meads et al, 2005c).

The same applies to regulation and governance. These expressions of modernising policies usually involve the establishment of external monitoring and quality control mechanisms that examine corporate performance for which there is collective interprofessional accountabilities. The enforcement of evidence based treatments by Health Maintenance Organisations in the United States and Sickness Funds in The Netherlands are obvious examples from the North. From developing countries of the South so too are the Municipal Training Committees of Colombia which accredit practice teaching programmes for seven health and social care disciplines and the combined Ministry of Health and Social Welfare in Bolivia which oversees all local practice teaching needs through its integrated human resources strategies. The implementation of these is monitored by an independent National Accreditation Commission for all first level health and social care.

New partnerships and national stewardship of social capital are the other defining features of contemporary health and social care systems in a global context. Once again innovations in interprofessional learning and practice development are widespread and plentiful. Frequently in fact, new partnership models of service are the prerequisite of such external donors as the Salem Foundation and Care International which look to fortify national governments that have struggled previously to exercise their stewardship roles and responsibilities. Cuba and Costa Rica have, for many, been role models driving forward their 'Solidarity' programmes on the basis of integrated health and social care developments that use such terms as 'Third Age' and 'Teaching to Learn' (rather than clinical conditions) to harness multi-professional and cross-agency energies. For modern Brazil, where the Kellog Foundation is a key sponsor, research as 'transdiscipline' is now promoted. Brazil, furthermore, is a country where past resistance to change has been such that one practice teacher told us it had been 'easier to change a cemetery than medical education'. The multidisciplinary integrated home care teams of Italian and Greek Regions benefit from being European Union pioneer pilots, while in Mexico the integration between professions seems more vertical than lateral in form, as trained community workers are used to identify and recruit potential future leading local health care professionals. Scandinavian cross-sectoral 'Care Chains', sub-Saharan generic 'Community Practice' and Malaysia's 'Train the Community' programmes for health and social care workers are just a few further illustrations of how interprofessional learning has become what one Sudanese medical teacher described to us as the 'soul' of the practice team and the spirit of its development. It is important that we begin by examining some of these global trends in more detail to discern the emergent IPE models.

Global trends: Learning together to work together

There is international recognition that the integration of services and collaboration of organisations and professionals within them should lead to more effective and efficient services (WHO, 1998: Mur & Van Raak, 2003). Demographic, epidemiological and therapeutic changes are occurring globally which necessitate team working and communication with others involved in health and social care across sectors, and new ways of collaborating are being enabled by technological advances. Decision making is routinely a multidisciplinary and therefore multiprofessional, although not always an educational process. In addition to learning how to work effectively with colleagues, health and social services professionals require new attitudes and skills that enable them to work with other sectors to provide comprehensive, high quality, continuous and personalised care which meets local needs (Alwan & Hornby, 2002).

There is growing appreciation of the important role interprofessional education can play in equipping individual professionals with these skills. By interprofessional education we mean education provided to more than one profession, with interaction as an important goal and increased knowledge, understanding and collaboration as an outcome (Barr et al, 2000) The sharing of knowledge is crucial to effective patient and service user care, and shared learning can lead to an increased understanding and respect of other professions' roles, abilities and knowledge (Funnell. 1995). This increased understanding can help to dispel negative stereotypes, improve perception of the roles of others providing care within a team and lead to an increased confidence in communication amongst professionals (Barr, 2002). Improving communication between different professionals and sectors should lead to improved communication between professionals and service users.

Two popular approaches to shared learning found in many countries across the globe are action research and problem-based learning, both of which are rooted in practice. Such approaches have been found to be effective in terms of outcomes such as improved attitude, knowledge and understanding amongst different professionals. Action research seeks to promote change through research and involves collaboration between researcher and researched in defining the research issue, planning the conduct of the research and deciding how to use and disseminate the findings (Morton-Cooper, 2000).

Problem-based learning, pioneered in medical education by such universities as Maastricht in the Netherlands and McMasters in Canada, emphasises the importance of students solving real patient or community problems, under the supervision of a more experienced professional (Barrows & Tamblin, 1980). Responsibility for patients as part of a team involved in patient care forms an important part of the assessment process within the medical education curriculum in such universities as Maastricht (Scherpbier, 2001) and McMasters and is reflected for social care by the approach of such new universities as Brighton and Anglia in the UK.

The position in the UK

In the UK, the promotion of collaboration and interest in interprofessional education has been a normative policy trend since the 1960s (Forman & Nyatanga, 1999). Since 1997, its development has been regarded as a key element in the 'modernisation' of health and social care (Haradon & Stainforth 2000), with proponents arguing that it facilitates the collaborative and partnership arrangements favoured in policy and is an essential element of the desire to provide a seamless service to users.

However, in the UK the critical issues to date have been around the identification of what interprofessional education means, and what a curriculum which embraces it would look like. This has included debates about when is the best time to introduce such learning into the curriculum. Yet to deliver change requires professional motivation (Frederickson et al, 1973). Consequently, the debate needs to move on to consider the issues of how to motivate professionals to work together, and indeed, for what purpose. This chapter describes IPE developments in countries which are reforming their health care systems and seeks to identify the drivers for collaboration and how these translate into different models of 'learning together to work together'. With a focus on developing countries where interprofessionality is integral to civil society and public service movements the aim is to identify the transferable learning for the UK and other 'first world' countries.

IPE: Fear and trepidation

In the UK interprofessional education has often met with suspicion. Fears of the introduction of a 'generic worker', of dumbing down and of loss of professional prestige and status have all been noted (Freeth et al, 1999). However, an examination of policy developments, supplemented by a review of the literature around interprofessional education developments across the globe, has not revealed any evidence to support these suspicions. Rather, where new multi-skilled professional profiles have been created (such as Italy's Health and Social Care Workers, Brazil's Health Agents and England's Mental Health Gateway Workers), these new occupations actually support traditional professional profiles, often acting as first point of contact for services.

Innovations in IPE: Learning from developing countries

Our international research study found that whilst developed countries such as Australia, Sweden, the Netherlands and Finland may be amongst those leading curriculum developments, some of the most innovative examples of developments in multiprofessional education and service delivery may be found in Africa and Latin America. In particular, developing countries are taking the models of action research and problem-based learning and applying them in innovative ways. Two different approaches to interprofessional education are described below as illustrations:

The African approach: Community based education

In many African countries the education of health and social care professionals is community based. For example, Moi University in Northern Kenya has developed the Community Based Education and Service (COBES) Programme. This takes the form of a collaborative partnership between the university and the local population. Students work with local people to identify needs and develop services or initiatives to address these needs. From year two onwards, all trainee doctors and nurses spend at least three weeks per annum located at a community health facility. Students do not simply have the chance to test and extend their skills outside of hospital; they also become integral to the process of identifying and responding to local needs. These have ranged from malaria netting, foster care and HIV education to new water jars, latrines and summer children's day care schemes. Community members are regarded as important members of a team who provide public health related services, including educational initiatives. Within Kenya, as a result, the concept of interprofessional education incorporates professionals working with communities, not just intra- and inter-professional working. Communities are involved in decision-making about health and social care initiatives as well as decisions about placements for trainee medical, welfare and health personnel. As in Ghana and Zambia, this collaboration has been successful in attracting support from non-governmental organisations, such as CAFOD and Action Aid as part of the sector-wide approach favoured by donors since the 1993 World Bank report on Investing in Health (World Bank, 1993).

In South Africa a new generation of multi-skilled nurses and community health professionals are being trained via interdisciplinary educational programmes. At Western Cape University, for example, a 'Shared Community Based Practice' approach is being piloted, which uses primary health care principles to target the poorest areas via interprofessional programmes. Shared Community Based Practice applies across the faculty and incorporates students of medicine, physiotherapy and public health. Operating in the fourth year of their training the students provide a service as part of their community attachment as well as undertaking local research and needs analyses. In Kwa-Zulu, Natal, Durban University's Community Rehabilitation model of health and social care education uses problem based learning approaches to integrate multidisciplinary contributions and extend local primary care services with trainee Occupational Therapists playing a central design role.

Similar programmes which combine interprofessional

education and action research are being promoted in Uganda, Nigeria and other parts of Africa with Sudan pioneering curricula design in community-based joint placements for nurses, doctors and pharmacists. Developments in Sudan (Box 1) illustrate the multifarious ways in which collaboration between trainee professionals and local populations can be encouraged as part of undergraduate education. While these are evidently an economic necessity in poorer countries, they do represent progress on IPE that few developed states have yet achieved.

Uganda provides an example of how epidemiology shapes local services and the educational model required to ensure that professionals are equipped with the skills to deliver them. The prevalence of HIV/AIDS means that services are provided at a number of levels, from the clan, to the village, the county and the district. At each of these levels collaborations between professionals takes place. The collaborative relationships range from those between doctor, nurse, community representatives, social care 'mobilisers', undertakers etc at the village level to public health officials, politicians and educational leaders at district and national levels. These relationships emerge as a response to the combined clinical condition and social need, and community-oriented education is therefore essential. Communities are key members of collaborative partnerships which seek to maintain health and well-being, as well as to respond to disease at the local level.

Latin America: The civil society based approach

The regeneration of professions and the relationships between professions is part of a widespread move to create new civil societies across Latin America, often in response to civil conflict and breakdown. Within Latin America professional development is regarded as a means of restoring public confidence, with professionals becoming role models for new societies. As such, many countries' national targets require services which are dependent upon collaboration between health and social care professionals. Within Chile, for example, as a result of the national health reforms, primary care clinics are being established which include up to nine different professions working together as a team to provide first point of contact services. In the South Metropolitan area of Santiago,

Box 1:
interprofessional education integrated across undergraduate curricula

In Sudan, interprofessional education takes many forms at the level of basic undergraduate education. First there is inter-school education, in which students from different schools undertake joint courses like physiology, basic skills, rural residency and field training. Secondly there are intra-school activities in which students of different programmes in the same school learn together. For example, the Faculty of Applied Medical Sciences at the University of Gezira has three such programmes: Health Psychology, Nursing and Anaesthesia, whose students learn up to 35% of the curriculum together (Ali, Elgaili, et al, 2002). An example of the third form is the Interdisciplinary Field Training Research and Rural Development Programme (Hamad, 1982). This is a three phase course in which small groups of students from medical and nursing schools are assigned to villages. Here the students work with local people to make a community diagnosis, prioritise health problems, and suggest and implement a solution through community mobilization. Finally they work together to evaluate the intervention. Such education aims to:

1. Reflect the importance of a team work strategy in the field of health;
2. Provide the maximum benefit for the community from the work of students from different disciplines;
3. Ensure that students learn from each other to draw a holistic picture of the state of health in the community;
4. Reduce the cost of the educational process and provide better utilization of the minimal resources available for education in a developing country,
5. Ensure that the longer established Medical Schools provide support to newly established schools (Hamad, 1982)

As well as the advantages of interprofessional education described above, it is also recognised as reducing the cost of the educational process. For Sudan as a developing country this is acknowledged as advantageous and provides an added incentive for its continuation.

Source: Mohamed Elhassan Abdalla, Faculty of Medicine, University of Gezira

for example, the Social Worker is a core member of the triage service, and the primary care centre team is led by a Physiotherapist with integrated multi-disciplinary education support from the Catholic University in the capital.

In Costa Rica, we found 8 national strategic level health priorities, with a strong emphasis on prevention. Local Strategy Groups were charged with implementing these priorities, all of which included educational objectives. Telemedicine was used in local primary care clinics as a means of ensuring that the strategic priorities in the 2002 National Health Implementation Plan were supported by team-based training protocols plans and adopted in local areas. The primary care clinics, or ebais, comprises a doctor, nurse practitioner, health technicians and host a variety of other health and social care professionals on a sessional basis. The primary care team all had access to the telemedicine facilities which linked them to both teaching hospitals for specialist expert consultations and also to provincial centres where primary health care and social care advice could be exchanged to facilitate the achievement of key strategic priorities.

Transferable learning

So what is it that makes interprofessional education and the integration of services work in these countries? Epidemiological, political, economic, professional and educational forces all inform and shape the structure of health and social care services and the educational models that support them.

Within the UK we are starting to see the organisation of services around long term conditions within some primary care organisations, particularly as a result of the new Family Health Services Contracts for GPs, Dentists and Pharmacists, and the revised three year curriculum for Social Work qualification (NHS Confederation, 2003: DoH, 2002). The organisation of services at this level is more akin to that found in many developing countries than the collaborative initiatives which have taken place to date in the UK. Whilst often excellent, these have tended to be independent and at the level of the individual General Practice or Field Work Unit, rather than across a locality. Consequently, the need to ensure that educational models reflect and shape the structure of health and social services is receiving increased attention and recognition in the UK. For example, new initiatives such as the NHS University Institute have sought to involve communities in defining and shaping their programmes and services (NHSU, 2004). The Institute aims to provide education which will 'enable staff to work more effectively across traditional occupational boundaries' (Loughlan, 2004) and respond to the needs of local areas whilst utilising local resources, including the knowledge, skills and capacity of members of local communities. This represents a shift away from the traditional discipline-based and experimental model of medical education towards the community development model of education found in many African and other developing countries.

Where next?

Understanding the forces which motivate professionals to work together is essential if education is to facilitate collaboration in service provision. Findings from our international research project have identified the following factors as representing important motivational forces for collaboration:

- Where education providers possess legitimised power to develop and manage services themselves they become accepted members of the political community for health and social services development. For example, universities in developing countries which rely on donors, municipalities and students for funding are often very pro-active in the development of interprofessional services, as well as educational initiatives;

- Education which adopts a values-based approach and incorporates the principles of redistributive justice and wider stakeholder participation should be enshrined within professional education if equitable services are to be provided. Where we have found these principles to be lacking health care systems have struggled, for example, to attract GPs to work in rural areas. The public can be left without access to basic health services (as seen in parts of Canada and Australia) and in social care in, for example, the Baltic States of Lithuania and Latvia, provision is dependent upon such emergency relief agencies as the Red Cross and Order of St John.

• Information technology can be used as a shared tool, accessible to all those involved in health maintenance and treatment (like the model described in Costa Rica).

As the many examples of innovations in collaborative practice and the educational developments supporting them presented within this chapter have demonstrated, interdisciplinary, interprofessional practice and learning are now global trends reflecting a cultural change underpinned in local, national and international policy.

So, what does all of this mean for those involved in practice teaching? It is essential that individual professions are equipped with the interpersonal skills necessary for team working and cross-profession collaboration. In particular, the created artificial barriers often found in 'first world' countries between health and social care, are gradually being taken down. By placing the client at the centre the necessity of providing a seamless service has been realised. Furthermore, health and social services are now routinely delivered in partnership with an increasing range of stakeholders from the statutory, voluntary, private and community sectors. Opportunities to involve all of these stakeholders in the design and/or delivery of services and educational initiatives are starting to be realised in the UK. There is much that can be learnt from other countries on this matter and, as demonstrated, especially from developing countries for whom such models are often a necessity (for example Uganda's response to the HIV/AIDS epidemic). However, it must also be noted that within the UK health professionals and the health sector as a whole would benefit from closer collaboration with the social care educational sector, where issues such as team working and community development have historically formed a larger element of training and development.

Within policy health and social care professionals are now conceptualised as team members as opposed to individual representatives of different disciplines and professions. Whilst the structural changes to accompany this conceptual shift are becoming more established the necessary behavioural change required is more difficult. And this difficult task falls to practice teachers whose role is to facilitate the learning of profession-specific and generic skills, as well as seek to develop professionals with a client-centred, flexible approach which enables them to work across a variety of settings, frequently as members of multi-specialist teams with new accountability arrangements, often to community committees or the like.

In the UK employers are now obliged to produce skills profiles for their staff to identify where further training and development is required to facilitate the interprofessional collaboration now enshrined in such policies as the National Service Frameworks around, for example, children's services, older people and mental health service provision. Consequently, professional education must ensure that professionals are equipped with relational skills, as well as an understanding of the contributions other professions can make to health and social care along with the necessary attitude to effectively fulfil both new differentiated and expanded role profiles. These principles are supported by the professional Colleges who now acknowledge the importance of shared learning/training around a number of issues and key skills. Professionals must be adept at working with their own profession and need to feel empowered to with other professions; with partner organisations, including the public, and with policy makers.

Identifying parallel developments in other sites through this brief description of developments in interprofessional education in developing countries demonstrates the potential for transferable learning. Such learning does not have to be limited to first world countries. Whilst context is undoubtedly important, learning about alternative models and processes which can be adapted, if not adopted, transcends context-specific boundaries.

Summary points

- The importance of interprofessional education as a means of equipping health and social care professionals with the skills needed to work effectively in team-based and integrated services is recognised across the globe.
- In the UK interprofessional developments are regarded as a key element of the modernisation of health and social care.

- International research has demonstrated that fears of interprofessional education leading to more generic job profiles are unfounded.
- Developing countries are applying interprofessional educational approaches in innovative ways which offer interesting models of relevance to the organisation of professional education in first world countries.

2
Group supervision for social work students on placement: An international comparison

Paul McCafferty

Introduction

The following comparison aims to advance ideas about the nature of international social work and to provide theoretical and illustrative material as a basis for developing my own practice in group supervision for social work students whilst on practice placement. I will compare the model that I have developed within my own agency (Partnership Care West, Practice Learning Centre) with a model that has been developed at the University of Haifa in Israel. I will argue that even an activity apparently so intimately linked to the socio-economic characteristics and culture of a given nation, must recognise the impact of the international arena, through a process known as internationalisation. I will discuss the usefulness and difficulties of an international comparison in social work. I will outline my own model, placing it in the local context of Northern Ireland. I will then outline the Israeli experience, discussing the local issues that effect practice in that country. I shall then provide a theoretical structure for comparing internationally and outline the similarities and differences at the mezzo, macro and micro level.

Discussion

While leaders in this field have historically been aware of developments elsewhere and have often been active at international level, recent rapid internationalisation has impacted on social welfare as much as other aspects of daily life, and now requires all social workers to place their local activities in a wider frame Lyons (2000). Social work has traditionally been seen as a local culture bound activity, specific to a given time and place; clearly there is an essential relationship between much social work practice and the nature, needs and requirements of the society in which the activity takes place (Lorenz, 1994 in Lyons, 2000). However in the concluding decades of the twentieth century, even countries that had previously been regarded as isolated or independent have been subject to the pressures of internationalisation.

Before continuing, I feel it is important to define what I mean by international and internationalisation? The Collins dictionary defines international as 'of, concerning, or involving two or more nations or nationalities'. Guzzetta (1990) defines internationalisation as 'neither exclusive importation of ideas nor exclusive exportation of ideas, but a clear understanding that the inter in international means reciprocal'.

Since the 1980s however, the term internationalisation has evolved and been replaced by the term globalisation. Dominelli and Hoogvelt (1996) argue that globalisation has three main features:

- The emergence of a global market principle.
- Flexible accumulation, and
- The internationalisation of the state.

A common feature of globalisation is a worldwide interconnectedness and interdependence that both characterises and is driving social change, Pinkerton (2002). Robertson (1992, p.8) calls this 'the compression of the world and the intensification of consciousness of the world as a whole'. All this has been made possible by the development of the communication media, the information superhighway and travel, making contact between different cultures more frequent and some would argue, more beneficial.

Usefulness and difficulties in comparative study

Pursuing the idea that this sense of interconnectedness is beneficial, Watts (1995) emphasises that learning from other countries 'is mutual, on-going and dynamic and can help us to advance the human condition'. Additionally, an international perspective can contribute to the shared understandings necessary to respond effectively to social problems, including alleviating poverty and combating racism, cultural imperialism and violence. Shared learning may help to find solutions and responses to what have thus far proved to be intractable human problems. An international social work perspective will be critical in documenting and recording human and social suffering and consequently new ideas to help alleviate distress and disadvantage might be found Watts (1995).

Healy (1990) supports this view, adding that social workers have added increasingly to what we know about issues such as mental illness, poverty, ageing, crime, child welfare, health care, substance abuse and community development and that this knowledge could inform the debate on these issues in the global market.

Furthermore, Healy (1990) argues that there are four main reasons for an understanding of globalisation vis-à-vis social work. Firstly, Healy argues that social work can provide an educated dynamic to resolving problems created by disadvantage and discrimination. Secondly, there is an increasing level of global interdependence and this has a direct impact on local social work practice. Thirdly, it is useful to have an international knowledge in order to practice locally. Finally, social work can take its place in the international arena alongside psychiatry, sociology and law etc., when it comes to resolving problems of a local nature.

In addition to this, Hokenstad (1992) suggests that social work has much to learn from the developing world's approach to tackling issues such as poverty and the increasingly despondent under class that western societies face. Hokenstad further argues that the responses to these problems need to be 'global in outlook and local in action', (1992, p.191). Hokenstad also claims that an international component in the social workers repertoire of skills helps social work liberate itself from cultural myopia.

Finally, having an international perspective might, in addition to the possibilities discussed above, be seen to reflect the very values inherent in social work practice - mutuality, respect and shared knowledge.

However, there are inherent dangers associated with globalisation. Firstly, there is a danger of ethnocentrism and racism. The danger lies in the fact that our analysis of others is based on our own worldview as opposed to looking at issues from the host culture. Secondly, using what we would define as our own normative framework implies superiority. This is especially so if globalisation is viewed as westernisation, and the export of capitalism. Thirdly, language, culture and social context can make shared understanding difficult. Finally, with globalisation, there is a danger of the reverse of more productive and helpful relationships emerging. The net result could end as polarisation, where we recognise one culture or group as totally different, or irrelevant Payne (1996).

Recognising these dangers and in an attempt to avoid them, Payne (1996) recommends that we develop what he terms a discursive formation strategy when it comes to exploring issues internationally. Payne advocates seeing the nature of social work as a collection of competing sets of ideas, presented as actions and concepts. The discourse about them forms social work. In this approach, we do not seek wholeness through one perspective. Instead, we value the discourse between perspectives as constructing a whole while exploring and valuing difference.

Issue for comparison

The issue that I wish to address, through a global comparison with another country, is group supervision with students at qualifying level whilst they are on placement.

I became interested in this particular issue in June 2002. When my colleague and I reflected back over the previous year's students and the quality and effectiveness of our individual supervision with them, we discovered several main themes in our thinking that we felt related to individual supervision; (for a fuller account of reflection see (Schon, 1983).

Firstly, it was difficult to equalise the power imbalance that existed between the student and us. This power imbalance existed on several levels,

- Teacher/student
- Perceived expert / non-expert
- Male / female
- Assessor / assessed.

Secondly, the students learning experience was being restricted by the one to one approach. There was limited room for alternative perspectives that could have enhanced the student's knowledge. Thirdly, the student would feel isolated and unsupported without peer contact. This could also lead to a block in learning and a feeling of being alone.

In addition to this, I also became interested in-group supervision due to the new challenges that practice teachers will face under the new degree in social work in Northern Ireland. From 2005, practice teaching will change dramatically. The role of the practice teacher looks likely to change and practice teachers/assessors will be required to provide practice teaching/learning in an innovative and effective way. NISCC are keen to develop new models for practice learning that are dynamic, progressive and that can meet the needs of students studying for the new Bachelor of Social Work.

Taking cognisance of this, I set about developing a model of group supervision that would begin to meet the changing needs of students and meet the challenges of the new degree. My model, outlined below, was developed by exploring and applying the theories of group work, supervision, adult learning and anti-oppressive practice theory, which I have outlined elsewhere McCafferty (2004).

The model

The model consisted of seven group sessions and seven individual sessions. These sessions alternated each week, so one week the students came together in a group and the next week the students were seen individually. Each facilitator retained the overall assessment responsibility for a designated student but the co-facilitator was able to add their assessment based on observations during the group.

Before the group started, we as facilitators met to prepare for the forthcoming session, feeling that this stage was crucial to the success of the group Douglas (1970). We checked in with one another on a cognitive and emotional level, ensuring we were fully prepared for the forthcoming session. We also ensured that we had divided the tasks equally between ourselves, thus ensuring we were modeling good partnership relationships for the students.

The group sessions themselves had a set agenda for each week and examined particular social work topics; these included contracting, evaluating process records, the theory and practice of social work, values in social work, self assessment and evaluation of skills, the importance of reflection in social work and portfolio construction.

The content of each session was purposely generic as each of the students was placed in different placement sites, with a different service-user group. Clearly, the content of the sessions does not have to stay the same and can be changed with the mutual consent of the facilitators and students. The point is however, that there was a main theme each week.

The group sessions all worked to a set format which meant that each week we began with an ice-breaker, which the students choose. This worked to get the members loosened up and created a relaxed and supportive environment. We then had a check-in, during which time individuals were given the space to discuss with the group, the interventions that they experienced with service users that week. Hillerbrand (1989) found that intervention skills are enhanced by the verbalization of the cognitive processes of students in peer groups. Conceptualization is more effective within peer groups than under the guidance of an instructor (Arkin, 1999).

We then took a break and the facilitators left the students by themselves. This was important as it gave the students a period of time together without being assessed and lead to a greater sense of solidarity and cohesion. When the group finished at the end of placement, the students themselves commented that this was one of the most valuable parts of being in a group.

We then spent time on the main topic for that week and explored this issue in depth. This process of exploration was completed by using role plays, presentations, group exercises, vignettes, group discussions and homework exercises.

At the end of each session, we set the students some work to do for the next session, which could also be used as evidence in their portfolios. All sessions lasted three hours. The entire process of group supervision was assessed and the students were made aware of this at the beginning of placement when they signed the supervision contract. When the group sessions finished, the facilitators met to debrief. We used a simple format to give some structure to this process and each week we looked at our thoughts regarding how well the session went, the actual facts of what took place and how the content could be improved and what we were experiencing on an emotional level, as a means of evaluation.

Context of the issue

This model of supervising students in groups, which has been developed at the local level, is of course set in the wider global and national arena. It is therefore important to consider these issues first, if one is to develop a sense of context. This too, provides the basis for comparison with the chosen international country.

It would be impossible to fully understand how my project functions in Northern Ireland without first considering the nature of the state in a society once described as the most violent in Western Europe, Campbell and McColgan (2002). Political and constitutional arrangements in Northern Ireland have always marked it out as a place apart within the United Kingdom. The Government of Ireland Act 1920 partitioned Ireland and left the northeastern counties a contested geopolitical space between catholic/nationalists and protestant/unionists. This resulted in a long and well-documented period of violence commonly known as the troubles.

Despite the complexity of the social structures put in place after this period, constitutional arrangements between Northern Ireland, the rest of the United Kingdom and the Republic of Ireland tend to be preoccupied with problems raised by the national question. In 1972 full legislative powers were removed from Stormont, which was the local parliament, and placed in the hands of Westminster in London. Described as Direct Rule this mechanism has meant that Northern Ireland was administered through a newly created Northern Ireland Office, headed by the Secretary of State and a small number of ministers.

Some attempts have been made to progress these arrangements, culminating in the creation of a devolved Assembly through the Belfast Agreement in 1998, which was preceded by a somewhat successful peace process, Campbell and McColgan (2002). This agreement has to a greater or lesser extent, addressed a range of issues, suggesting openness to progressive reform and an emerging culture of human rights.

Unfortunately, at the time of writing, the Assembly is currently suspended and Direct Rule re-imposed. However, before the Assembly was suspended, it did make some major contributions to the way in which Northern Ireland manages its own affairs

One major contribution with relevance to social work was the creation of NISCC. Previously, the Central Council for the Education and Training of Social Work (CCETSW) was responsible for ensuring the standardisation of social work education. However, with the creation of the devolved Assembly with the power to make decisions effecting health and social welfare, NISCC was created to take over the role of CCETSW.

NISCC is a statutory body established by the Health and Personal Social Services Act (Northern Ireland) 2001. The aims of NISCC are to provide protection to those who use services, promote high standards of conduct and practice among social care/workers, strengthen and support the professionalism of the workforce and promote confidence in the sector NISCC (2003).

Relevant to this discussion, is the fact that NISCC has been provided by government departments with funds for the improvement of social work education. One of the areas for which these funds are available is to increase the number and improve the quality of practice placements. More specifically, NISCC contract directly with the Practice Learning Centre here at Partnership Care West to provide practice placements and contribute to the development of practice learning.

It is interesting to note in the context of my discussion about the effects of globalisation on local issues, that the very concept of a contract and contracting in social welfare appears to have been influenced at global level, not at local or national level as it would seem.

The globalisation of the economy has had an enormous impact on the British welfare state. Like other parts of the national economy, the welfare state has had to respond to the pressures for greater international competitiveness. It has done so by becoming a site that could provide capital for accumulation purposes and restructuring to allow the private commercial sector a greater role in welfare provision. Thus, globalisation has affected the structural framework and organisational culture of social work.

One consequence of these changes is that British statutory social work has become more fully integrated into the market economy. Statutory Social Services now contract work out and have had to cede their role as service providers to the voluntary and commercial sectors and become primarily purchasers of care. This shift has drawn both the statutory and voluntary sector into the business world via the medium of contracts Dominelli and Hoogvelt (1996).

The emergence of a global market principle involves the imposition of a new categorical imperative, namely global market efficiency, upon the domestic supply of goods and services. This sets the parameters for the privatisation of the welfare state and creates the conditions for a new relationship to be established between state and providers of welfare. This became known as contract government, which has been crucial in facilitating the welfare state's move from being a resource provider to a purchaser of services from provider units. The provider unit in this instance is Partnership Care West, whose actions are contractually defined and who are accountable for their behaviour.

Thus, one can see a direct link that the global emphasis on efficiency has on the welfare state at national level and the delivery of services at local level. In a drive for greater efficiency and innovation the state, represented here by NISCC, has purchased the services of Partnership Care West's Practice Learning Centre and secured that relationship with a contract. This contract has in turn, been influenced by global market efficiency principles.

Relevant practice from the other country

This section outlines a similar project of group supervision in another country. The comparison is with group supervision of social work students in their second and third years in the Undergraduate Social Work Programme at the University Of Haifa School Of Social Work in Israel

In terms of context, Israel, like Northern Ireland, is a relatively new state. It was established mainly by European and Russian Jews who, having suffered persecution and exile from their own countries, finally had their dreams of establishing a political and geographical entity realised in 1948 when they established a home land in Israel Milton Edwards and Hinchliffe (2004). Over the next decades, Israel would overcome a variety of political and economic obstacles and survive several wars. The Jewish population would swell from about 500,000 in 1948 to over 5,243,000 in 2001, which was the result of natural growth and in-migration from many nations.

While Zionists asserted that all Jews share a common nationality, the practical challenge of uniting an incredibly diverse and often traumatised population in a new state was enormous Chomsky (2003). A consciously created culture, education, military experience and language were devoted to the task. Despite this, Israeli society continues to be stratified along the lines of ethnicity, class, religion and ideology Harris (1998). Further distinctions, having evolved within the particular social, political, religious and economic context of the Jewish state, continue to challenge national unity and consequently, the ideological basis of Israeli society Gold (2002).

With regards to social work, according to Israeli social work law 1996, if one wishes to practice as a social worker in Israel, it is necessary to first gain professional certification. One must then register in the social workers register (Pinkas Haovdim Hasotzialim) (Publications Department, English Section, Ministry of Immigrant Absorption).

To become a social worker, one must undertake a Bachelor of Social Work or Master of Social Work degree. All of Israel's major universities offer social work degrees at both the Bachelor and Masters level. The licensing and accrediting authority for these degrees is the Council for Higher Education, which is a statutory body, responsible for accrediting and authorising institutions of higher education to award degrees Hagshama (1998).

Regarding the University of Haifa programme, students graduate after three years of Social Work study, reaching the Bachelor of Social Work (BSW) degree, which serves as a licence to practice. The curriculum includes thirty-two hours of class work per semester and nineteen and a half hours of fieldwork per week during the second and third years. During this time all students in the programme undergo group supervision in addition to individual supervision. In the second year, group supervision is devoted to individual intervention and in the third year to group and/or community intervention. Group supervision addresses issues related to the particular method that the student is being asked to deal with in practice but it also involves using groups and group processes as a medium of teaching and learning Arkin et al (1999).

According to the overall model, the second and third year is divided into three phases in which three distinct supervision methods are applied. The three phases are to consist of:

1. The formative phase,
2. The working phase, and
3. The ending phase.

Within each phase there is a set content that the student must learn, as well as the use of different processes to enable the student to learn. Each phase also requires the supervisor to undertake different roles. For a fuller outline of this model see Arkin (1999).

Comparative analysis

It has been argued that a tentative framework for comparing social work in different countries can be developed using the notion of social domains Huston and Campbell (2001). This entails adopting the view that the interplay of distinct domains or spheres of activity can explain social life. Domains can be thought of as a distinct layering of experience that determines action, Layder (1997). Although these are interlocking and mutually exclusive, no particular domain is the prime mover in terms of influence.

Three types of social domain are helpful in explaining and comparing social work practices globally. These are the macro, messo and the micro domains. The macro domain refers to large-scale international processes directly effecting nation states and indirectly effecting local social work practices within them. The messo domain can be viewed as the site where relationships between nation state, welfare regimes and social professionals are played out. The micro domain alludes to the specific activity of everyday social work practice, where academic discourses become transformed into practice wisdom, Huston and Campbell (2001). I have outlined the similarities and differences in each domain below.

Macro

Similarities

Both countries have at some point in their history been affected by the policies of Britain and America.

Britain maintained a presence in the Middle East up to 1948 and continues to have a presence in Northern Ireland.

The USA has had a political interest in both countries and has helped negotiate peace settlements in both countries i.e. the Good Friday Agreement in Northern Ireland and the Road Map for Peace in the middle east.

Both countries are relatively newly developed nation-states. Israel was founded in 1948 and Northern Ireland in 1921.

Both countries occupy contested geopolitical spaces.

Both countries exercise disproportionate power over world affairs compared with their geographical size and population.

Both countries experience high levels of violence.

Differences

Northern Ireland has managed to establish cease-fires from most of the groups who endorse violence to achieve political gain.

Another major world power, Russia was involved in the political life of the Middle East through its support of the Palestinians.

Northern Ireland is only beginning to be effected by the immigration of Central European peoples.

Meso

Similarities

Social work education is state sponsored, accredited and standardised

All social work education in Israel is university based. Northern Ireland is moving towards this system.

Social work practice is focused on the socioeconomically derived, physically and mentally disabled people, children, victims of political violence, and older people

Differences

Northern Ireland is only just moving to the BSW. Northern Ireland is doing away with the Masters programme.

Israel has a more culturally diverse population.

Northern Ireland is only recently beginning to have members of ethnic minorities move here.

Social work education in Northern Ireland is undergoing dramatic change.

Micro

Similarities

Fieldwork experience is seen as a vital component in social work education.

All students are supervised whilst on placement.

Group supervision is available to students.

Differences

Supervisors in Israel are University linked and accredited by the University.

Supervisors in Northern Ireland are known as Practice Teachers and are agency based.

All students in Israel undergo Group Supervision as well as individual supervision.

Students in Northern Ireland only get Group Supervision if the practice teacher chooses to work in this way.

The model in Haifa endorses weekly group supervision as well as individual supervision.

The model in my project has group supervision one week and individual supervision the following week.

The model in Haifa has three distinct phases (1) the formative phase (2) the working phase (3) the ending phase.

The model in my project sees each session as a separate entity unrelated to the next session.

The Haifa model places an emphasis on personal growth and development through an experiential process.

The model in my project places an emphasis on learning skills, acquiring knowledge and identifying values.

The model in Haifa has a pass or fail attached to the group supervision process.

My project sees the group as one part in the assessment process and does not have a pass or fail to the group section.

Implications

It is evident that the Haifa model of group supervision is more established and refined than my own. There is a long history of group supervision in Haifa, which has been tried and tested over a long period of time. Finding this model through a global comparison has been of excellent benefit to me and I intend to transform my own model in several areas.

To begin with, I intend to view the sessions as a continuum, with the formative, working and ending phases as outlined in the Haifa model, and not as single entities with a separate focus. Traditionally, each of my sessions began with a check-in about individual placement issues. Despite the fact that this did provide some useful insight into social work issues, I have recently begun to view this section as a placement management section, which could be completed at a different time. Discussions often focused on the practicalities of the placement or placement specific issues and the other members appeared excluded.

Additionally, the group did not have a sense of beginning, middle or end or experience the different feelings associated with each of these stages. This would have been useful because having experienced these feelings, the students could have tuned-in more effectively to the feelings their service-users may have at each stage of the professional relationship. In turn the students would have a better skill, knowledge and value base with which to practice empathetically.

I also feel our roles as facilitators need to develop. Historically, I think we have been overly concerned with the intellectual development of the students as opposed to their emotional or personal development. Looking at the Haifa model, the reader can see that the supervisor's role is to enhance the emotional world of the student and provide a model for good practice, as well as ensuring they have the necessary knowledge, skills and values to practice.

Additionally, I need to consider whether or not to make it explicit to the students that the group is assessed. At present it is stated at the learning agreement that supervision is one means of assessment but this seems to get lost somewhere in the process. For example, some students are very quiet in the group and add little to exercises, discussions and role-plays. Until now, I have tended to let this pass, arguing that we have other methods of completing a more holistic assessment. However, if an aspect of social work is about communicating and engaging, surely students need to be able to do this in a variety of settings, including groups and that their ability to do this needs to be assessed.

Finally, I feel that with the new BSW being introduced in Northern Ireland with an 85 day placement in the second year and a 100 day placement in the third year that our model will lend itself more easily to developing the experiential type of group endorsed by the Haifa model. At present there is enormous pressure with placements being so short and an almost manic emphasis on the portfolio, leaving very little room for a more experiential group. With longer placements, more time can be spent on personal growth and developing a professional identity. I therefore intend to do more sessions.

Conclusion

This has been an exceptionally rewarding comparison to do. For the past few years I have been supervising students in groups. I always felt this was an excellent way to supervise students and that they gained a lot from the experience. Recently however, I have wanted to develop this model by looking at how other professionals have approached the issue. I therefore decided to undertake a global comparison and I feel that this has been of great benefit to me.

As a result of the global comparison, I have been able to formulate new ideas, gain greater insight into other models and at the same time, learn something new about our fellow social work colleagues in another country. Additionally I feel our model has become more organic and dynamic. My comparison has also increased my confidence in the professional rigour of my model and given me the assurance to present this model as an alternative to the more traditional one to one supervision approach usually favoured in the British Isles.

3

Understanding African cultural values in practice teaching

Wilson Muleya

Introduction

This chapter looks at African cultural ways of learning. The focus is on highlighting some of the challenges faced by practice teachers outside Africa who train students from Africa. Western literature (such as Asante, 2002; Graham, 2002) shows how social work practice has developed mainly as an intervention grounded in Western eurocentric culture. As Asante illustrates, the profession has given little thought to the nature of practice with non-white clientele. Similarly, there is very little on enabling better training for non-white European students. Practice teachers may need to understand the students' specific cultural learning strategies to be able to facilitate quality practice learning experiences. Ecological and systems theory are drawn on to highlight influential patterns of socialisation within African culture, and how early life experiences may later influence how students learn.

The discussion begins by looking at the purpose of practice placements and goes on to address two questions: 'What is Culture?' and 'What is African Culture?' A discussion on ways of learning encouraged within African culture then follows. The final section looks at challenges for practice teachers and suggests an approach for practice teaching students on placement.

Practice placement

Social work practice placements provide students the opportunity to demonstrate their competence within a learning environment. Learning on placement is a significant aspect of professional development. Practice placements provide the environment for students to develop their professional identity as they become socialised into the professional role. Students gain practical experience of working within an agency. This builds on students' own existing knowledge. At the point of taking up placements, students will have what Eraut et al (2000) identifies as 'Codified knowledge' and 'Personal Knowledge'. The former consists of theoretical knowledge gained at college/university which is codified, stored and accessible from print media such as books and publications. The latter consists of cognitively stored knowledge or internal factors that students bring to practical situations that enable them to think and perform (Eraut et al 2000). The authors regard learning as a process by which personal knowledge is acquired.

On placement, learning occurs through a process of transferring of knowledge (Eraut, 1997). Transference will involve both personal knowledge and academic (theoretical) knowledge. There is a growing body of western literature that looks at how adults learn (Rogers, 1996; Kolb and Fry, 1975), and at enabling adult learning (Race 2001). The literature shows that different individuals may prefer particular ways of learning based upon their previous experiences. To enable learning, the focus within social work placements is on how students are helped to integrate and apply theory to practice, whilst incorporating social work values within a practice environment.

The environment within which learning occurs has implications on how individuals learn. Social work practice placements take place within work environments that may offer very structured and coordinated frameworks for service delivery. These include government agencies regulated by state laws. However, some work environments are flexible with activities coordinated around agency objectives, principles or ethos. These include voluntary agencies (non-governmental organisations). Students undertake placements to demonstrate practice competence regardless of the nature of the agency. Both external and internal factors are likely to affect how individuals learn and demonstrate their competence. External factors include agency policies, procedures and guidance on service delivery. Internal factors include 'culture' in so far as this offers a framework for socialisation and making sense of one's reality. The process of how individuals construct what is reality for them will have implications on how they learn. A further discussion is presented latter in this chapter.

How students use their internalised learning experiences (Personal Knowledge) within the environmental context of the placement, will affect how they learn. However, the nature of the professional relationship between the practice teacher and the student equally plays a significant role in this learning process. The success of the placement will depend on how the relationship is developed, how roles and responsibilities are defined and clarified, how power differential is managed and how the practice teacher and student understand each other's learning strategies. For non-African practice teachers training African students, outside Africa, an understanding of how African culture might influence students' learning is important to enable effective learning.

What is 'culture'?

The term 'culture' can simply be understood as a way of life of a group of people. The term is generally used to refer to a commonly shared understanding of activities or behaviour among people who belong to an identifiable social group. Within literature on Anthropology, Geertz (1973, p.89) has used the term to imply

> historically transmitted patterns of meaning, embodied in symbols, system of inherited conceptions expressed in symbolic form by means of which [people] communicate, perpetuate and develop their knowledge about and attitudes towards life'.

Other authors, such as Weisner (2000), use the term to refer to shared values, beliefs, and activities organised in daily routines where individuals' interactions and experiences have emotional meaning. These cultural factors play a significant role in influencing individual behaviour. The behaviour occurs within cultural boundaries. Cultural boundaries are important for sustaining a sense of cohesion for a given group of people (Youngelson et al, 2001). Within this context, individuals obtain validation for their own understanding of the world, derive a sense of moral security from their relationships with each other and obtain emotional reinforcement for what it means to be human (ibid).

Similarly, Berger and Luckman (1966) define the term 'culture' by showing how social factors shape individual's sense of personal reality. They regard this sense of personal reality as a construct developed along typifications, or collectively shared constructs and beliefs commonly subscribed to within a social group. These factors are seen to define community, within which the values and norms are transmitted as guidelines on how to live one's life and what to expect from others. Hence, Thompson (1998) uses the term 'culture-specific' to refer to this environmental nature by which individuals' patterns of thinking and feeling become construed.

Therefore, to understand how culture affects behaviour, individuals' actions are best understood by gaining an insightful understanding of the latent, not so obvious, factors in play or what lies beneath the surface. McLeod (1998) argues that it is the underlying web of meaning and inherited conceptions that are symbolised and expressed in external behaviour. Seen as such, 'culture' provides a framework within which group members share a collective sense of belonging and an understanding of their interactions within a specified social environment.

Influence of external factors

Cultural groups do not exist in isolation, but are influenced by different external factors arising mainly from capitalist demands for global trade. Inglehart (2000) shows that although, 'culture' has not been spared this influence, throughout the history of social development, culture remained influential in determining behaviour. Inglehart (2000) draws on literature from development studies to suggest that culture has played and continues to play a significant role in the development of society. He identifies two arguments. One by Weberian thinkers (Fukuyama, 1995; Harrison 1985, 1992, 1997; Huntington, 1996) who view modern political and economic behaviour of societies as drawing on enduring cultural traditions. The second, by modernisation thinkers (Inglehart, 1990, 1997), regards development to occur as a result of coherent cultural shifts away from traditional value systems. Inglehart argues that both these claims are true. To demonstrate this, Inglehart utilises data from three waves of the World Values Survey (WVS) consisting of sixty-five societies containing 75% of the world's population. Inglehart makes the point that a society's historical orientation remains consistent when effects of economic development are controlled.

In African and other developing countries, capitalist economic advancement has had an impact on traditional values, norms and living arrangements. The most significant being the emergent of urban communities (Ranger, 1993). Different ethnic groups now live together and share the same geographical space. With these economic changes, traditional 'culture' has had to adapt whilst retaining characteristic features. Studies, such as Chibuye, Mwenda and Osborn (1986) and Akuffo and Akuffo (1989), on child upbringing practices in Zambia, show that traditional family system values pervade African society. The studies show that urban family system is characterised by the presence of people in households who are offspring of neither husband nor wife, but tend to be relatives of the couple. The responsibility for child upbringing and socialisation in urban setting continues to be a shared one between both biological parents and other members of the extended family. Although within these arrangements the roles performed by parents, children and extended family are well defined, some individuals may choose to emphasise certain aspects of traditional values and not all of them. Similarly, with varying environmental conditions, individual experiences may differ as individuals adapt to new ways of interacting.

What the above analysis shows is the view that contemporary societies are characterised by distinctive cultural traits that have endured over long periods of time. These traits have an important impact on social behaviour, particularly in so far as influencing how Individuals develop culturally specific ways of learning and survival skills relevant for their respective social environment. This point has significance in supporting an argument for practice teachers to gain an understanding of students' cultural ways of learning. This is particularly important where a student brought up in Africa undertakes a social work practice placement outside Africa supervised by a practice teacher from a different cultural environment.

What then are the main distinguishing African values that might determine ways of learning in practice teaching? Before addressing this question, it is worth looking at what is meant by 'African Culture'.

'African culture'

Africa is a vast continent (with over fifty countries) whose inhabitants speak a range of different languages. Ethnic groups include black Africans (mainly occupying Sub-Saharan region and West Africa) and Arab speaking groups (mainly in North Africa). Given this diversity, is there a distinctive African Culture?

There is consensus among some African scholars that certain characteristic ways of cognitive thinking are influenced by African culture. Lassiter (1999) in his discussion paper that surveyed and assessed the writing of selected African scholars (mainly from the sub-Saharan region) on the subject of 'Africaness', summarises that the scholars identify categories and processes of cognitive thought seen to be unique to Africa. This characteristic feature provides a way of thinking based on a restrictive socio-cultural setting (Lassiter, 1999). This implies that by interacting within a defined cultural boundary, individual behaviour is subjected to a form of environmental conditioning (Lassiter, 1999) or what Nyasani (1997) has referred to as cultural streams. Within literature on behavioural approaches, theorists have shown how patterns of behaviour when reinforced are sustained and those that are discouraged become extinct.

Historically, societies in Africa are agrarian. African environment has encouraged social interactions centred on close collaboration among individuals in their efforts to survive. This has provided a basis on which patterns of socialisations and social interactions have developed. Despite influences from western capitalist activities, African communities have retained identifiable features on socialisation. These features include:

- Identifiable hierarchy of authority
- Problem-solving structure and mutual reciprocity
- Importance of survival values (over self-expression values)

The above features will determine how an individual in an

'African culture' learns. Regular reinforcement of these features will encourage a particular learning strategy. These features are discussed in more detail in the next section. The focus here is on understanding how the systems of roles and practices functions, and how the expectations and belief systems sustain a certain pattern of learning. Emphasis is on core African values. Graham (2002) makes a distinction between core or classic cultural values and popular cultures, by emphasising that core values underpin and shape individual interactions, whereas, popular cultures tend to be reflective of current trends in society.

Ways of learning

To explore how culture may influence learning, let us begin by taking the birth of a child as our starting point. A child is born into an existing family system of interrelated networks. The child, referred to here as 'Malaika Mutu' (translated as 'Angel Person') assumes a position within the family system. Malaika is born into a family with two older sisters. We know from natural science that at birth, Malaika is born with no prior social knowledge and skills, but rather has a clean slate. What Malaika learns is dependent on how the family system transmits knowledge. The transmission is guided by values and norms that define acceptable and non-acceptable behaviours, and in turn serve to hold the family system together as a functional unit.

Learning takes place predominantly through the informal process of socialisation. As a member of the family system, Malaika will experience different interactions as s/he develops into an adult member of the family system. African cultural environment may encourage learning drawing on the following:

Identifiable hierarchy of authority

African culture offers a clear and distinctive hierarchy of authority. As individuals join the group through birth, their position is clearly defined. Within the prescribed family position, Malaika grows up respecting elder members of the social group. Depending on the child's gender, specific roles are prescribed. As a male child, Malaika will command more authority than that of his two older sisters, the older he gets. For Malaika, the process of learning is such that he is encouraged to take on roles of decision making while his sisters will be aligned more towards caring roles. The women tend to gain this power through activities aimed at affiliating themselves with men as opposed to meeting their own needs and asserting their own views. Although the female members mainly undertake the role of child carer, the men actively participate as authoritative figures that reinforce community values and discipline within the family. It is worth noting here that functions of families are coordinated and held together by women and that increasingly, more families are headed by females who are also the main income earners.

When Malaika presents deviant behaviour, this will have implications for both birth parents and adult members of the extended family. As a network of family members, the behaviour of one member affects that of others. Deviant behaviour is seen to reflect a failure not only by the child's biological parents but equally the elders of the extended family in their role of socialisation. Malaika, like other children, is assumed to be undergoing a process of socialisation. Malaika is yet to reach the stage when s/he will become accepted as a responsible adult member of the family system and society. Until this status is attained, children are not seen as wholly responsible for their behaviour.

Hence, children are regarded not to be knowledgeable enough to participate actively in decision-making. They are excluded from this process. It is the responsibility of adults to make informed decisions on their behalf. Exclusion from decision-making does not mean children are not part of the overall process, as the expectation is for them to implement (usually without questioning) the decisions arising from the adult decision making network. Value of respect for adults underpins this process. When being informed of the decision, children are discouraged from maintaining constant eye contact with adults as this is construed as challenging adult authority, or merely being disrespectful. Malaika would not openly disagree with decisions made by the adult network. Where this need arises to disagree with adults, Malaika may elicit support from close adult members of the family system such as grandparents, uncles and aunties, or cousins, to represent his/her views (advocate).

An understanding of this process of decision-making is

important for understanding what will become Malaika's cognitively internalised concept of power/authority. Therefore, to understand Malaika's displayed behaviour, one ought to adopt a broader perspective that takes into account other factors affecting the observed behaviour. These factors may not be so obvious to an outside observer. For Malaika, the implications are such that until s/he reaches adulthood, s/he will expect to be informed of final decisions, made by adults, about important life events. Malaika will be expected to behave and perform roles according to the wishes of not only the birth parents but other adults in the family network and community. This will change, depending on the child's gender, when Malaika reaches adulthood. At that point s/he will be consulted and made part of decision making.

However, Malaika may not always abide by the core tradition of respecting authority. Should Malaika rebel, the family may force him to conform. Failure may lead to isolation with no contact at all with the family network. The system does not easily accommodate disloyalty. In modern arrangements where families live more in smaller nearly nuclear units, rebellious behaviour might be addressed using strategies relevant to prevailing environment conditions. The pressures to conform are therefore reduced but the expectation for younger family members to respect elders remains present.

Mutual reciprocity and problem solving

Mutual reciprocity and respect rests on the assumption that society exists as a holistic entity. The belief is that if one gives assistance to another individual in need, either emotional or practical (food) the favour will be returned when the giver faces difficulty at a later stage in their life. This serves as a form of security and trust which develops into a strong mutual bond as the favours are returned. Traditional African society is structured in a way that promotes community as opposed to individual interests. As a network of interrelated social ties, families tend to be supportive of their members. The implication for individual members is to think and act in ways that promote consensus and discourage confrontation. Malaika growing up in this cultural environment learns the importance placed on supporting one another.

When problems arise, the system encourages a problem definition that is family (system) based. The problem lies within the family and not with the individual. Therefore problem solving takes the form of a family system activity. Problem solving may involve convening a family meeting attended by adults to look at alternative actions. Family meetings are held to share ideas, experiences, and to identify resources and support. A desirable action plan is agreed for implementation. The action plan may involve agreement on clearly identified individuals (including the young person) to implement the plan. Through the hierarchical structure of authority, decisions are disseminated to relevant family members for action. Where a problem can not be resolved in a manner that maintains stability (harmony) within the family, the person causing the problem can be asked to leave the community.

For Malaika growing up in this cultural environment, s/he will implicitly learn to think and act in ways that promote family consensus. Malaika learns a strategy that relies on adults to effect desired changes. The assumption here is that adults understand what is best for children therefore change led by adults will lead to desired change in the children's behaviour. As a young person unhappy with aspects of life at home, Malaika would be inclined to influence parents by seeking support from other adult members of the family system who would in turn, advocate on her/his behalf to influence parents to change their approach. This becomes a learnt process that gets desired rewards. An understanding of these processes and the dynamics on which they thrive is important.

Importance of community survival values (over self-expression values)

Another feature of 'African Culture' is the importance given to community responsibility and interdependence. This implies a collective approach whereby individuals regard themselves as members of a community and make decisions in the light of the needs and priorities of their social network. These actions as reflected in such arrangements as that of care for vulnerable members (children, elderly and disabled).

The elders within traditional settings are seen as valuable members of family units who are both knowledgeable and wise.

The assumption is that these people have served during their active lives to take care of their family and in old age it is the younger generation's responsibility to care for them. As knowledgeable adults, they remain part of the family unit and actively contribute to the socialisation of younger members of the family. By emphasising community survival values, African culture provides a support system that offers security and dignity to elder family members. The younger members are discouraged to behave in ways that promote self expression. This is seen as deviant as it moves away from traditional norms that underpin communal living.

There is research evidence to suggest that changing socio-economic environment has led to changes in the way teenagers perceive their role. Research in southern Africa (Mukoboto 1993; Cremins 1984) indicates that although teenagers value kinship relationships, they are taking more and more of an individualistic approach in their efforts to survive. However, as Akuffo and Akuffo (1989) warn this may alienate them from the elderly members in their families and society.

Construction of reality

The point to note regards the above identified ways of learning, is that the learning process is influenced by how reality is constructed. McLeod (1998) makes a useful distinction on how cultures in Western Europe and non-European countries construct reality by referring to the sixteenth century French philosopher Descartes' separation of the world into two types of entity, namely the Mind and the Body. McLeod's discussion shows that the mind consists of ideas, concepts and thoughts (with no physical identity), while body consists of tangible and observable entities. McLeod shows that in different cultures, people have different ideas about the fundamental nature of reality. He argues that people in Western countries generally hold a dualistic view of reality (mind and body), while those in African and other non-Western societies do not. For him, this difference explains the development of different terms and concepts in Western society, which refer solely to psychological phenomena such as depression and anxiety, which are terms that are difficult to define in African culture. Reality, in African culture is experienced as a complete whole where the mental and the spiritual are understood as aspects or facets of a single unified reality, rather than as separate domains (McLeod 1998). The inclination is to define psychological phenomena along spiritual terms, where an individual is seen to be possessed by 'a bad spirit'.

These differences in construction of reality are relevant for advancing the argument made in this chapter that cultural factors determine how individuals learn by constructing the view of what to them is reality. How this knowledge is transferred and applied to different settings to acquire personal knowledge will, determine how the student learns on practice placement.

Identified strengths for practice teaching

The above discussion has highlighted the following strengths for practice teachers to build on as they enable students to transfer and adapt knowledge to their practice learning environment.

African culture encourages a learning strategy that assigns power to individuals in authoritative positions. This provides individuals with a concrete representation of authority. As a student on placement, Malaika may assume the role of 'a learner' who is not yet to be fully socialised into the role of social work practitioner. Hence, the learning strategy may take the form of being less proactive, less critical and reliance on the practice teacher, to undertake roles as dictated by his position (status) within the organisation.

African culture regards social relationships as serving specific purposes. Relationships developed between children and male adults focus on discipline, while those with female adults are around meeting caring responsibilities. Relationships with other influential adults are used as support while those with elderly members (i.e., grandparents) tend to be viewed as resources of wisdom and advise on everyday life events. Therefore, Malaika will bring to the placement, transferable personal knowledge and skills on interpersonal relationships.

African culture regards individuals as parts of a system. This has implications for problem solving. Malaika may define presented problems by focusing on the group as opposed to individual members. Although this gives a holistic view, this might result in failure to individualise service-users. Malaika's initial responses to presented problems may be skewed more towards group based interventions. However, Malaika will bring to the placement, analytical skills in problem solving that see presented problems in their totality.

An approach to practice teaching students on placement

Kolb's (1984) Experiential Learning Cycle shows that learning occurs in four stages namely; experience, reflection, conceptualisation and experimentation. Davys and Beddoe (2000) in their application of Kolb's learning cycle argue that learning extends beyond 'doing' and should be considered to include feelings and ideas, generalisations and theories, and future use and adaptation. They propose a model of student supervision that they developed from the work of Ford and Jones (1987). Through a process of reflection, their model allows for an internalised process of critique and monitoring or self-supervision.

It has been argued earlier in this chapter that learning that is culturally determined involves cognitive processes. Adult learners have valuable past experiences of learning from which they develop preferred learning strategies. African culture encourages a particular learning strategy. The approach proposed here, builds on the positive aspects of learning identified earlier, relevant for enabling African students develop professional practice. The approach draws on Davys and Beddoe's (2000) view that learning extends beyond doing. As illustrated in figure 1 below, students bring to the placement personal knowledge, which knowledge they use to explore, implement actions, and reflect, on both the outcomes of the interventions and the process itself. The discussion below highlights specific features of African culture relevant at different stages of practice learning. Practice teachers may need to be aware of and / or incorporate the features, wherever identified, within the learning environment they provide students. The approach serves as a guide for good practice. It is acknowledged that not all students on placements outside Africa will have had the same experience of African culture, hence may not find this approach useful.

Figure 1
Incorporating African Cultural Values in Practice Teaching

		Stages of learning on placement		
		EXPLORATION (beginning stage)	**ACTION** (learning stage)	**REFLECTION** (assessment / ending)
Features of African Culture affecting learning	**AUTHORITY**	Relate to and differentiate; (1) how authority is structured within placement setting, (2) decision making process	Difference of opinions (student & practice teacher) Self –direction Risk taking Risk Assessment	Self assessment
	RECIPROCITY	Supervision relationships Team relationships/working patterns Transference	Approach to work	Distinct professional role
	COMMUNITY SURVIVAL VALUES	Professional standards Social work as collective responsibility	Approach to professional practice Skills development	Professionalism

Exploration

The exploration or initial practice placement stage begins with practice teacher and student developing a teacher-student relationship. Student brings to this relationship their own learning strategy and personal knowledge gained from past experiences. To enable learning, the initial stage should involve exploration of what the student brings, acknowledging areas of differences, strengths and those that might need addressing. The exploration stage should identify an approach to practice teaching that will compliment and build upon the student's existing knowledge. Figure 1, outlines three features that might affect learning at this stage.

Exploration vs authority

African culture has a clear structure of authority. The practice teacher may explore with the student, the nature of authority within the agency. This should highlight how power is structured, how decisions are made, who contributes to decision-making and how outcomes are communicated. The focus should be on enabling the student to relate to and differentiate how agency authority is structured in comparison to their own culturally informed understanding. How the student interprets these structures will affect how they learn, particularly how they interpret actions. Clarifying the agency's decision-making structure will provide the student with a clear framework of reference.

At this stage, power, gender and cultural differences between the practice teacher and the student should be explored and acknowledged. In African culture, individuals command authority on the basis of their gender and position/status within the hierarchy of authority. Where barriers are identified which may hinder effective communication, an action plan for overcoming these should be explicitly outlined and an agreement made on how the plan would be implemented. Exploration should involve an open discussion on the hindering factors, and preferred ways of overcoming them. Challenging the student's views without exploring alternative ways of enabling better communication (that encourages learning) may not necessarily prove to be an effective strategy. Adult learning in African culture allows considerable discussions before agreeing on a course of action.

Exploration vs reciprocity

Students will bring to the practice teacher – student relationship personal knowledge of social interactions grounded in the cultural norm of reciprocity. The student should be enabled to transfer this knowledge in a constructive way. This knowledge is relevant to draw on, in clarifying various professional relationships (interactions) that the student may develop particularly when working in partnerships. This would include multi-agency and collaborative work. The student will share responsibilities within the supervision relationship and within different relationships developed with team members. Exploration ought to clarify the different roles, responsibilities and expectations of team members at different levels of the agency's structure. This will provide a defined practice setting that reflects the student's experience of a structured system of relationships. The differences between student's interpretation and those of practice teacher should be explicitly outlined and addressed within supervision.

Exploration vs community survival values

Social work is a profession that adheres to professional values, standards and codes of practice. Practitioners do not practice in isolation. They follow professional guidance. Exploration should focus on drawing on the student's implicit personal knowledge of interacting in ways that promote community survival. This knowledge provides a structural framework for understanding the implication for both following and not following professional standards, and the importance of sharing the collective responsibility. Social work is a profession that increasingly relies on effective information sharing with other professionals involved in meeting service-users' needs. The student will bring to the placement personal knowledge and experience of interacting in ways that emphasis community survival values. Through practice supervision, the practice teacher may enable the student to transfer and apply this knowledge to practice in order to demonstrate competence in adhering to professional values of social work.

Action

The action stage or the 'doing' phase involves learning where students put into action their internalised knowledge. Placements provide different learning opportunities within which students can demonstrate their competency. The following features may affect how students intervene and provide services:

Action vs authority

African culture allocates actions (and power) to individuals on the basis of their position within the hierarchy of authority. This may have implications for the student in relation to how they communicate what they may regard as actions they may or may not do. The student may have difficulties in vocalising difference of opinions. As highlighted under exploration Vs authority, individuals have different expectations. Two issues may arise here. Firstly, the student's approach to problem solving may focus on working with parents and adults to implement actions on behalf, and in the best interest, of the children. This approach may not suit all cases. The student's learning strategy may regard young people as members of wider social networks who are undergoing a process of socialisation, and not socialised at a level where they can effectively engage in decision-making. Secondly, the student may not be self-directed, take less risk and may not take the same approach for assessing risk, as that of the agency. The learning strategy encouraged within African culture takes a holistic systems approach. Students may not necessarily focus on individual needs but identify group needs. This approach will focus on outlining the whole picture and describing the interactions taking place and may not effectively isolate individual needs.

The role of the practice teacher is important here. Depending on the agency setting and legal responsibility, the practice teacher may use constructive criticism to enable the student to evaluate how their approach might distort how they assess need and manage risk. Supervision sessions are preferred for both addressing this issue and for enabling further student learning. The focus being on enabling learning as opposed to minimizing the student's internalised cultural knowledge. In supporting student learning, the practice teacher may equally develop their own awareness of the student's experience of authority and how this may affect how they implement actions.

Action vs reciprocity

The knowledge and experience of engaging in reciprocal interactions is useful for multi-professional working. Practice teaching should focus on drawing out the student's knowledge of interpersonal relationships and how individuals compliment each other's actions. Given that students will work as part of multi-professional teams, they will rely on others' actions and contributions. The student should be encouraged to assess how effective their interactions with other professionals are and how these can be linked into the agency's procedural regulations.

Action vs community survival values

The principles that underpin the value of maintaining and sustaining community continuity are transferable skills that practice teachers can focus on to enable students to apply to their placement environment. This may guide the student's actions in contributing to the organization. Within the practice tutorial, student should be encouraged to use these skills to act in ways that promote the work of the placement agency.

Reflection

The reflection stage involves a continuous process of self assessment including how the student undertakes assigned work within the placement. Although the discussion that follows is presented in separate headings, there are no clear-cut boundaries where reflection on authority, reciprocity and community survival values begins or ends.

Reflection vs authority

This requires practice teachers to challenge student's use and interpretation of presented issues on the basis of their own cultural experiences. Students should reflect on how their understanding of authority structures might not necessarily apply to that of their service users. Within practice tutorials, practice teacher should offer opportunities for the student to assess through a reflective process, how power structures affect their actions. This should encourage the student to identify any areas for further learning.

Reflection vs reciprocity

Attention here ought to be on getting the student to assess effectiveness of the professional relationships they have developed. This should enable the student to identify aspects of their professional relationship roles that they find easier to undertake and those that might not be that straight forward. Learning can then occur where the student is encouraged to build on existing skills. As discussed earlier, in African culture a system of reciprocity is encouraged among individuals. This form of interaction may not necessarily be the norm within the placement. Reflection on this will enable the student to adjust accordingly.

Reflection vs community survival values

Here reflection should be used to encourage student to identify how their own actions might be impacting on the placement's work. This should involve addressing student's understanding of how their own work adheres to professional codes of practice and placement procedures. Emphasis should be on enabling student to assess how they actions contribute to the continuity of the agency's work.

Conclusion

This chapter has highlighted some of the ways in which an understanding of African culture by practice teachers training African students, outside Africa, may encourage use of practice teaching approaches that take into account the influential role played by the student's own culture in determining their learning strategy. African culture encourages a learning strategy that is led by adults exercising considerable influence over the learners. Learning takes the form of a 'top to bottom' approach. Hence, the learning strategy tends to be that which seeks guidance from authoritative figures, whilst promoting group cohesion. An understanding of these processes is relevant in determining how students training outside Africa transfer personal knowledge to their practice learning. Where practice teachers adopt a practice teaching approach that takes this into account, they are more likely to facilitate better and effective practice learning. This discussion has recommended an approach that places the student at the centre, and not only acknowledges their existing personal knowledge but endeavours to drawn on this when practice teaching.

4

Back to the future: Evaluating a project to disseminate practice learning and teaching in Ukraine

Steve Ambler and Adrian Black
with Tatanya Tartachnyck

Introduction and Context

In September 2000 the authors were invited, via the TEMPUS European Development project, to visit the Chernihiv Law College (now an 'Institute' – we use both terms – see below: 'Conclusions') in northern Ukraine to teach on a five-day module at Masters' level. This was designed to help those delivering social work education in their Oblast (region).

Anglia Polytechnic University was a partner in this project, and continues through TEMPUS to be a partner with Higher Education Establishments in Ukraine. One of the authors had undertaken a similar visit in Kyiv (Kiev) three years previously. Both the authors had extensive experience of practice teaching and learning in the UK as practice teachers and lecturers. One had been Chair of the East Anglian Organisation for Practice Teaching (EAOPT), and the other had been Chair of the National Organisation for Practice Teaching (NOPT). One was a training manager in a large statutory agency, and the other was a university Practice Learning Coordinator with working connections in the voluntary or non governmental organisation (NGO) sector. The authors had previous extensive experience of working and teaching in tandem, from a common value base. This mix of experience and skill was the main reason for the invitation for the authors to undertake this visit.

Our visit represented the final TEMPUS input at Chernihiv Law College. Unlike other large cities in Ukraine, notably Kyiv and Lviv, Chernihiv had very few teaching visits from UK social work educators. However, some of the College's social work lecturers had undertaken their professional training on a TEMPUS supported course in Kyiv.

The major content of the five-day module focussed on practice learning and the development of assessment and work-based learning systems. However, 'woven' into the content, at the request of the group, were sub-themes of adult learning theory, teaching methods, teaching techniques and presentation skills. TEMPUS aims to disseminate social work education throughout Europe, and contemporaneous and immediate evaluation of the teaching block demonstrated its success to those ends, and that the participants valued the learning.

Following our initial visit in 2000, the Director of the College expressed a strong interest in our returning, after an appropriate time span, to evaluate the effect of our input on their teaching and learning systems and to assist with planning further developments. In 2002 we were successful in obtaining a grant from Anglia Polytechnic University (APU) via the Research Assessment Exercise (RAE). This allowed us to fund a small research project to assess the impacts of our previous visit. In addition, we were testing the validity of short-term development projects against our hypothesis that longer-term local 'partnership' working would be a more effective way to initiate and support professional developments.

We considered such research important for those involved in social work education in the UK and other European countries, in order to evaluate the effectiveness of working in newly independent post-Soviet countries that have recently experienced great structural change at social, economic and political levels.

Our research posed the following questions:

* Do our UK systems, values and practices transfer to other cultures?
* Were the stated aims of TEMPUS with regard to 'dissemination' of practice appropriate?

- Have we managed to sow fertile seeds rather than impose potentially inappropriate or damaging systems?
- Have our learners been able to develop their practice as a result of our visit?
- What, if anything, is needed next?
- If TEMPUS (and similar projects) are about facilitating change, what evidence of this has there been in the context of our visits?

This paper will reflect on our initial teaching visit and presents the subsequent research findings. It is an account of how two experienced social work educators (but with very limited research activity) learned from their experience when they went 'Back to the Future' in Ukraine.

First Visit: September 2000

Our first visit to the Chernihiv Law College, in September 2000, as previously stated, was via the TEMPUS Development Project. We were invited to deliver a five-day intensive module focussing on the following subject areas:

- Adult learning theory
- Practice learning values
- Practice learning – Who? What? Why? Where? When? How?
- Identifying and developing learning placements
- Training, developing and supporting practice teachers
- Models of practice learning / roles and responsibilities
- Placement planning, induction, learning agreements, endings
- Power relationships, teaching, learning and assessment
- Standards, evidence (triangulation, Direct Observation) and failing students
- Learning and teaching techniques / presentation skills.

The whole process was supported by building on the knowledge and experience gained by one of the authors through a similar previous teaching visit to Kyiv.

One of the issues which we addressed was that of constructing the agenda for our teaching. Bridge (2000) describes a similar experience of teaching in Eastern Europe, and suggests that the ownership of agenda setting should rest with the group of learners, and that the teachers should be responsive to this. However, previous experience of one author was that of trying to 'pick up the pieces' following a previous teacher who had used this process, abandoned given structure, and inadvertently 'pinched' all the ground to be covered the next week, whilst leaving a curriculum gap in a certificated course! Our module too was part of a certificated Masters programme. Thus we were clear that the content, negotiated between college, TEMPUS and ourselves, had to be delivered.

From this starting point we were determined to reconcile the two factors of given curriculum and 'starting where the learners are' (Knowles, 1980; Rogers, 2002).

Whilst the research findings indicate that the learners' agenda was more keyed-in to actual tasks of their working lives, it was easily agreed and accepted by the group that the given curriculum was essential. Indeed this provided a coherent structure to the module and, therefore, to the larger programme as a whole.

The prevalent learning and teaching environment in post-Soviet higher education institutions is on the whole traditional in nature with classic didactic lectures as the norm. The concept of 'androgogy' (Knowles, 1980), i.e. the teacher as a facilitator of learning, was somewhat alien to the group. Conversely, our mode of delivery was very interactive and therefore we had to be particularly sensitive to the group's reaction to our rather different teaching style and learning methods. In this respect as a 'teaching team', although our practice backgrounds were very different, we have been heavily influenced by the work of Brigham (1974), Freire (1972), Morrison (1993) and Rogers (2002). As a result we share a common value base that is firmly committed to adult learning principles and that these are universally transferable, indeed this aspect has formed one of the major hypotheses of our research.

Two major learning domains of the group were to enhance their presentation skills and learn new teaching methods. The group consisted of college social work educators, practice teachers and service managers from both state and voluntary sectors. These were individuals who were in key positions that would enable them to 'disseminate' new ideas and practices, one of the key objectives of the TEMPUS Project and other similar programmes. We therefore felt it essential that we demonstrated a full range of teaching techniques and used a variety of resources that would be easily understood, transferable and readily available in Ukraine. This latter point of resource availability is particularly important given the general lack of funding allocated to resources in higher education.

Our overall teaching strategy mirrored that of Catherine Sawdon (Doel et a, 1996) who suggests a 'tool kit' of action techniques for social work practice teachers, her taxonomy is easily transferable to class teaching situations, she suggests following groups of techniques:

- Hardware such as IT, audio, video, OHP, etc.
- Written and printed materials
- Graphic material, such as charts, diagrams, pictures, cartoons and illustrations
- Experiential – role-play, sculpting, simulations, etc.

All of our teaching was undertaken via interpreters. Therefore using graphic materials and experiential techniques became significant when delivering the learning. Given the general lack of resources we were unable to use information technology based approaches such as PowerPoint. Indeed there was even a lack of flipchart paper and pens – what little was available we used sparingly to provide permanent records of issues and activities that could be typed up for later use. We had prepared some overhead projector acetates, mainly pre-translated, for factual and visual presentations. In the main, however, we used a chalkboard for simple data, presenting models, inter-active work and dispensable feedback, giving us a different teaching discipline from our usual styles. This was a positive use of simpler technologies.

In our first session with the learning group we formulated a shared agenda that reconciled the given curriculum with the group's learning needs. This was achieved via a group exercise where we charted their stated learning needs and 'wove' these into the 'fabric' of the set programme. Our use of such metaphors was a persistent thread throughout our teaching. Metaphors were used as a vehicle for sharing and elaborating our experiences and as a medium for common understanding. We are indebted to our friend and colleague David Sawdon, who has skilfully demonstrated use of metaphors in NOPT Annual Workshops, and on training events.

When using metaphors we were careful to check for common understanding, given differences in culture and language. The visual aspect of many metaphors enhanced our ability to transcend language barriers. Indeed, the process itself of checking meaning between learners and teachers further embedded the learning. As a result, the method of using metaphors became common learning currency offered by teachers and learners. A prime example of this was discussing marginal or failing students who had not previously presented learning issues. We use the metaphor of a swan: very serene, apparently calm on the surface of the water; but frantically paddling below to make headway against the current. Our group members were quickly able to relate this metaphor to learning processes.

What Surprised Us!

Initially we were somewhat taken aback at the influence of the prevalent model of didactic teaching. At times there was a reluctance to engage in group activities. However, when 'encouraged' to undertake some collage work in groups, attitudes did change dramatically. After this experience they were able to reflect on the value and purpose of this method and having to work alongside those with whom they had at times disagreed professionally. We initiated an exercise that resulted in the group identifying a common value base with regard to practice teaching and learning. Consequently we explored links and comparisons with NOPT (2000) Code of Practice for Practice Teachers and the value statements in CCETSW's (1996) rules and regulations for the Diploma in Social Work. This process, exploring a common value statement that could be used with Practice Teachers and students was a risky strategy (what if we had nothing in common?). In reality, it provided a firm foundation for learning – and certainly supported our hypothesis that social work values can be universal. Our experience here echoed that of Cornwell, et al. (1999), particularly around student centredness.

We were also anxious about raising issues relating to anti-discriminatory practice. However there was a remarkable commonality at a conceptual level, demonstrating some 'deep' prior learning on the part of the group. Our experience in this respect somewhat differed from that of Bridge (2000).

One author was pleasantly surprised at the group's willingness to address teaching and learning issues. This contrasted sharply with a similar visit to Kyiv three years earlier when a group resisted this, wishing to concentrate on learning social work practice.

Overall we were very impressed with the group's levels of enthusiasm to learn despite the often difficult circumstances within some of their working environments. Quite often they were low paid, not paid regularly and experienced very adverse working conditions. One individual who worked in a prison was regularly operating in a climate of violence and anti-social work culture. Despite this he was committed to providing appropriate and worthwhile learning experiences for social work students.

The research

The research was conducted using three different tools:

*   Evaluation Questionnaires (for participants in the original learning programme)
*   Structural Interviews (for individual participants in the original learning programme)
*   Focus Groups (for groups of people with similar roles – for example, lecturers/tutors, practice teachers, student social workers)

This use of different data collection instruments allowed us to collate and analyse both quantitative and qualitative data, in order to draw some empirical conclusions whilst also being able to generate narrative and creative feedback and ideas for future development. Robertson and Dearling (2004) describe how potential insights provided by either model of data collection can be missed in the other, and that much social research demands a mixture of methodology, as we used.

The Evaluation questionnaires

These were designed so that learners could reflect on their learning from September 2000 and see how much impact this learning had had on their practice in social work education since then. This was elicited in two sections – firstly the learning objectives of the 'given' teaching agenda, and secondly the learning objectives of the agenda compiled by the learning group. Additionally, the questionnaires were also designed to evaluate how effective a number of the aspects of teaching had been for respondents as learners.

Scores were ranked on a four point scale (1 = not effective, 4 = very effective). Thus the median ('satisfactory') score was 2.5.

For each of the three sections, respondents were asked to provide short narrative comments on the three learning objectives/aspects that they found most useful/effective.

The structured interviews

These were designed to go into more depth with a smaller number of individuals from the original learning group – to discuss how learning from that week may have affected the participants' practice in social work education since, alongside other changes and developments.

Whilst it was out intention to use this format with original group members in their workplaces, it proved difficult to see them on their own as complete management and staff groups wanted to speak with us. Additionally, we soon discovered that a few of the questions were not generally pertinent (e.g. section on use of Learning Agreements, as there is a prescriptive Government-led system).

Therefore in practice we used the structured interview framework as a tool for leading discursive interviews with a number of people – drawing out what is happening in the field of practice teaching and learning in Ukraine, strengths, weaknesses and aspects for change/development.

Focus groups

The focus groups were set up for groups of people with similar jobs/roles in the practice learning arena.

Four topics were suggested for each of the groups, which met for one hour. The groups used a model of 'strengths/weaknesses' and 'keep/change' (Doel et al, 1996) to examine these topic areas. We did not take part in the discussions – but facilitated, recorded, kept time and led a debriefing session afterwards.

This gave us a good qualitative picture of what is working well, what needs to change, and building up a development agenda for the future.

Ethical issues

We had identified some ethical issues in undertaking this research:

- Anonymity and confidentiality – local, college, publication of material;
- Reporting back – accountability;
- Power of interpretation process
- Ensuring common understandings
- How do we ensure we do not get 'the answers they think we want to hear'?
- Setting the framework with the college (as an interested party).

We shared these issues with our colleagues in Chernihiv Law College and with all participants in the research – exploring best ways to minimise/counteract any problem areas. Throughout we endeavoured to maintain a learning culture of openness, honesty, freedom to express any views – positive or critiquing – in order to both evaluate effectiveness and to develop an agenda for future activity.

Evaluation questionnaire: Part 1

Overall the rating scores with regard to the usefulness of the set agenda were high for all areas, ranging from 4.0 to 3.1, the most useful in the subsequent work undertaken by the respondents can be grouped as:

•   Social work/practice learning values
•   Learning and teaching techniques
•   Presentation skills
•   Assessment issues.

Whilst all areas were rated relatively highly those with the lower scores, when related to usefulness in subsequent work were:

•   Failing students
•   Relationships, power and learning agreements
•   Training, developing and supporting practice teachers.

However, undertaking the research provided us with further contextual knowledge. Such knowledge highlighted some of the assumptions that we had brought to our first teaching visit and therefore to the content of the research questionnaires. We ascertained that structurally, learning agreements and the development of practice teachers are not within the domain or influence of our learners' practice. We also found that there is not a culture of failing students in practice (although they may fail academically). As a result these content areas were obviously of great interest to our learners, but perhaps not so relevant from a current practice perspective. However, the interest shown in 2000 was a good indicator to raise possibilities when discussing a developmental plan for future work.

The UK experience of academic and professional practice being integrated both holistically in assessment is at the beginning stage of development in Chernivhiv, academic assessment being prevalent. We introduced the concept of a practice curriculum in our initial visit but our research highlighted that our learners not been able to implement such a learning system to date. However, in a recent visit (July 2004) the development of the

Practice Teacher as a formal assessor of practice has been put on the agenda for future joint work.

It was to our particular surprise (at the beginning of our research visit) that the concept of learning agreements was not more highly ranked, given the interest and enthusiasm for this particular topic we had encountered from the original learning group. Again, this has remained 'on the agenda' as an aspect for possible future development.

We also learned that there is not, as yet, a regular practice teachers' training course in the region, indeed formal systems for supporting and training practice teachers are only at the embryonic stage. At present formal meetings between all local practice teachers and the college staff take place every three years! However, our research has indicated that the links between individually assigned tutors, practice teachers and agencies is very strong. As a result of our second visit, the college is considering organising a more frequent developmental forum. Indeed it became apparent through discussion with all parties that these three topics remained important, and could be the focus of future joint activities as practice learning systems develop in the Chernihiv Oblast region.

The four most highly rated areas perhaps reflected the practical aspects of delivering work-based learning, which is not entirely surprising as we did ask what had been most 'useful' in their work. The lower rated ones focussed on certain systems and processes which, as became evident to us, were largely in the control of others, for example College and Government Ministry.

The high rating of the values content supports our original hypothesis (prior to our teaching in 2000) that practice learning values, adult learning principles and social work values have some universality and practical transferability.

In our initial visit in 2000, we were delighted at the group's willingness to develop and to test out new learning and teaching techniques, and presentation skills. Little did we guess at just how much change this learning would facilitate. On our research visit in 2003, we heard how the social work school at the Law College in Chernihiv had changed its teaching methodology and how a new Social Work Education Programme in another college had designed its teaching methodology in line with the approaches learned on our module. Even more startlingly, we saw in action how a rural school

40 kilometres away had changed some of its teaching culture from a didactic to an interactive approach, due to working in partnership with one of our students.

We were shown collage work, symbolism, drawings and diagrammatic presentations produced by social work students in the college, since our previous visit. One of the lecturers had been inspired by the module to set up a 'Student of the Year' competition where a short-list of five students shared their talents in front of 400 other students and staff (and two researchers from England!) by using drama, quiz and project presentation – quite an innovation for the college.

Evaluation questionnaire: Part 2

These objectives were set as a result of an 'idea-storming' exercise on the first morning of the original module in 2000, as part of agenda setting for the week. Therefore some of these objectives were of quite personal/specialist interest to individuals/small numbers within the group.

Thus, as the evaluation showed, there was more variation between the perceived usefulness of these objectives than of those in the 'set' agenda, although the scores were still high (range 3.9 to 3.0).

The 'most useful' comments showed more marked clustering; but the depth of a number of individual comments demonstrated just how important it had been to take on these personal learning objectives. Examples included: 'Due to this knowledge we developed more tight links with NGOs'; 'I use statistics (information from the UK) in my lectures'; 'A volunteers programme was implemented in the orphanage in Chernihiv'.

The highest ranked objectives were:

- New methods of social work education in higher education
- Groupwork with clients
- Governmental Agencies and NGOs – roles and responsibilities
- Social work and social policy in the UK
- Information about voluntary organisations in the UK

The higher ranked areas were perhaps relevant to most of the group, in contrast some of the lesser ranked areas reflect more specialist interests, e.g. working in prisons. The average rating was 3.5 (out of 4), indicating that most of the learning was highly applicable to practice, either directly or through transferred learning.

Objectives ranked lower were:

*   Statistics (information from the UK)
*   Management of social work
*   Practical work in the UK
*   Case study working with those who work with prisoners

Although the scores for these objectives were somewhat lower as a group score, some achieved high scores for individuals to whom the topics were work-relevant, particularly 'management' and 'working with prisoners'.

Evaluation questionnaire: Part 3

Unlike Parts 1 and 2, where evaluation was targeted specifically to post-course utilisation, this section was designed to evaluate the overall effectiveness of the teaching on the 2000 module. We had requested, but did not receive, an analysis taken (in Ukrainian) at the end of our teaching week in 2000. We were told that this evaluation had been very positive, which tied in with a group exercise, undertaken on the final day of our teaching to evaluate the immediate reflections on achievement of the learning objectives.

In this third part of the Evaluation Questionnaire, we asked how effective fourteen aspects of our teaching had been for the individuals as learners. All aspects were rated very highly, with scores ranging from 4.0 to 3.7, as below:

1. The information given	3.9
2. Adult learning principles demonstrated in the teaching	3.9
3. Modelling of social work values in the teaching processes	3.8
4 Valuing the contributions of the learners	3.8

5. Incorporating the learners' learning needs into the module agenda	4.0
6. Comparing aspects of social work and practice learning in the UK to those in Ukraine	3.9
7. Teaching as a pair	3.9
8. Teaching using interpreters	3.7
9. Using different models of teaching	3.9
10. Learner participation in the process	3.9
11. Use of humour in the teaching	4.0
12. Overhead projector slides	3.9
13. Handout material	3.9
14. Organisation of the module	3.9

Given the similarity of scores, it is difficult to differentiate these areas for evaluative purposes. However, the 'perfect' scores for 'incorporating the learners' agenda' and 'use of humour' were borne out by the authors' anecdotal evidence. Similarly, we were not surprised at the slightly lower score for 'teaching using interpreters'; which was primarily a (very successful) method of overcoming a barrier, rather than a teaching method in its own right.

The Structured interviews

The structured interviews were designed to highlight how the learning from our original teaching week may have affected practice learning in social work education in Ukraine since, alongside other changes and developments. Our hosts (Chernihiv Law College) were also keen to obtain feedback from their placement providers regarding ongoing relationships and in particular to identify areas for further developmental change. We originally intended to interview several members of our 2000 learning group; however due to their geographical spread this proved to impractical. We therefore focussed on interviewing key individuals from placement agencies and key academic personnel in the college. The focus of the interviews centred on current practice, its strengths and issues for developmental activity.

The interviews were designed to elicit qualitative information to expand on the data provided by the Evaluation Questionnaires, and to incorporate other perspectives (than our original learners) into the research. We designed a framework of question areas, knowing that it would emerge that different areas would be more relevant for different interviews. These 'templates' were used for questioning and recording purposes, with particular areas expanded upon during interviews where appropriate. The methodology was that described as 'semi-structured interviews', (Punch, 2005, p.169) in which common threads could be expanded in individual responses.

Thus the structured interviews provided two major areas of information to add to the reflective and evaluative feedback we had received from our learning group:

1.   Information (and therefore understanding) about current systems, power relationships, and practice: strengths and weaknesses.
2.   Issues and areas for development and a potential agenda for change and future partnership working.

Nine structured interviews were undertaken, five in social work agencies, three with Chernihiv Law College staff, and one with two ex-students who had graduated in 2002. Whilst the interviews had been intended for single person responders; most of the interviews involved more than one person, as staff groups got very interested and active in the process!

Findings

1.   *Information*
     •   There was no evidence of formal agency policies or procedures about practice learning. However, learning outcomes and the agency/college agreements were used as procedural guides.
     •   The Chernihiv Law College has procedures in a programme handbook and a placement handbook. These are referred to in the contract/agreement about the placement, which emanates from the college and is agreed by the agency.
     •   There were no separate learning agreements, although some respondents, from both college and practice, felt that this was an area to be developed. There were a number

of references to the Ministry procedures for practice placements, and that there was no room/need for separate agreements within this framework.

- There was no evidence of formal interim reviews; but respondents appreciated the visits of tutors, who supported with general guidance.
- The 'final report' was in the form of a placement diary, compiled by the student and verified by the practice teacher, which then became the basis of an academic piece of work by the student.
- There was no formal training for practice teachers. Respondents from all positions felt that the meeting once every three years between college, agencies and practice teachers was a good developmental forum.
- One respondent (practice learning coordinator from Chernihiv Law College) said that in September 2000 it had been harder to find placements; but that now placements were asking for students.

2   *Ideas for development*
- Several agency respondents felt that more resources were needed, including 'motivators' for agencies to take students.
- One agency respondent felt that there should be a move from 'observational practice' by students (passive), to more 'technical practice' (doing).
- There were a number of respondents who wished to see more meetings between college and agencies to provide ideas and suggestions for development.
- One college respondent wanted to ensure that students were used as learners within agencies, not as cheap labour.
- One college respondent wished to practice teachers being actively involved in assessing and marking of competence.
- One agency respondent felt there should be a specialist Practice Teacher role, and several commented that they were practice teaching in their own time, as it fell outside their contract.
- Additionally, two respondents felt that practice teachers

should be paid for the task.
* Four of the respondents felt that there should be formal training for practice teachers.

These structured interviews gave some factual detail, which was useful to us as external workers and to the college particularly. They have also supported and added to the other research methods used in indicating agendas for future action by all parties. A number of the respondents at the time mentioned to us that the interview process itself had given them ideas, and helped to crystallise their thinking around these issues.

Feedback from all agencies was very positive about their relationships with Chernihiv Law College, and about the commitment to practice learning. The theoretical knowledge that the students brought with them from college was held in high esteem. In particular, there was praise for the staff at the College, and as to how they approached and involved the agencies in the processes of practice learning.

Focus groups

We chose to run some focus groups as part of the research in order to get qualitative data, from a variety of stakeholders. This was to be less structured and therefore more likely to engender creativity and to bring in areas that we might have omitted due to our lack of sophisticated understanding of local systems, culture, language etc. It was a clear and deliberate message that this action research was about supporting our Ukrainian partners in having power to determine and plan their own agenda and solutions.

Punch (2005) describes how focus groups should be relatively unstructured, to 'stimulate people in making explicit their views, perceptions, motives and reasons'. Thus whilst the researcher has a pre-planned list of topics and questions, she or he becomes a facilitator or moderator rather than an interviewer, relying on the process of group interaction to gain a richness of data. This is how we designed the focus groups, having sets of topics as starting points for each type of group.

Three focus groups were facilitated; with lecturers and tutors, with students (from three different cohorts) and with agency representatives (including practice teachers and students). Apart from identifying the impacts of our original teaching visit, Chernihiv Law College were enthusiastic about gaining the views of their stakeholders regarding practice learning systems, processes and relationships. They also wished to use this feedback in their bid to gain Institution status, and also identify any changes that could be made.

Impacts of the teaching visit, September 2000

There was a consensus of opinion that:

- More active and creative teaching methods had been used.
- Practice teachers had understood the value of adult learning theory in underpinning their teaching.
- Small groupwork had been initiated as a teaching method at the college.
- Consciousness had been raised regarding the importance of practice learning.
- Individuals had re-examined and reflected on their learning and practice.

Perceptions of the college (from agencies and students)

- The students who undertook their placements were of a high quality.
- The college was considered to be a centre of excellence for preparing specialist workers.
- There was good liaison and contact with the college staff, who were in the main accessible.
- The college was prepared to work in partnership, and generally agencies felt this was an equal relationship at a personal level.
- However, systems, paperwork, handbooks etc. were college generated and controlled.
- The students were provided with a wide practical experience, which enhanced their job prospects.

• Generally, the students' presence motivated agency workers.

Potential for change

• More agency participation in the development of handbooks etc.
• Regular development / training and support sessions for practice teachers.
• Development of practice teacher training and formal qualification.
• More information about students before they arrive, this would enhance the process of matching students to placements.
• A more rigorous assessment of practice. Particular interest was expressed regarding the development of assessment tools and resources.
• More higher-level management placements were needed.
• Placements needed to be longer.

Overall the data from focus groups complemented the data obtained from the evaluation questionnaires and structured interviews. Again, the perceptions of the focus groups were re-assuring to the College in terms of stakeholder perceptions, and contributed to the ongoing process of development and agenda setting.

Conclusions

The authors initially posed questions regarding the validity and usefulness of international initiatives in social work education such as TEMPUS. Our research findings indicate that adherence to and implementation of adult learning principles and values provided a firm foundation for learning. This learning was in many instances transferable to the future practice of those who participated. Also highlighted were the unforeseen positive consequences of our visit, in particular how our teaching and learning techniques were adapted to a primary school setting. On our return in 2004 we learned that Chernihiv Law College had achieved Institution status and we were thanked for our contribution to this process.

We believe that longer-term partnership is essential and viable as Chernihiv Law College (now Institute) had received minimum input via TEMPUS regarding practice learning. Indeed our original teaching visit was the only one; as a result further developmental areas were identified i.e. the setting up of forums for academics and practice teachers, practice teacher training and the development of more comprehensive and rigorous practice assessment systems. Given that the UK's experience has evolved over many years with relatively large resources, Chernihiv Law Institute sees the importance of utilising such knowledge and experience in order to develop their own practice learning systems at pace in response to the major social, economic and political changes they are currently experiencing.

It was interesting to note, in the light of recent policy shifts in the UK, how much positive emphasis was placed by the agencies on the need for practice teachers and assessors to be professionally qualified. In this respect we too agreed with this valuing of social work qualification in the teaching and assessment processes.

In our opinion, based upon the findings of this research it is essential that the vast reservoir of knowledge and expertise developed in Western Europe continues to be made available to our Ukrainian (and other) colleagues. Sadly our teaching visit was the final practice learning TEMPUS project hosted by Chernihiv Law College.

The larger centres of learning such as Kiev had more substantial and comprehensive social work education projects; the intention was to 'cascade' this knowledge to other areas of Ukraine. In some respects this was successful as a number of academic staff at Chernihiv Law College were social work graduates from Kiev's Mohlyar Academy, thus the dissemination of academic social work knowledge was being achieved. However, there had been little input on practice learning prior to our visit; inevitably the status of social work knowledge outweighed that of practice competence and skills. Our visit of 2000 was therefore a catalyst to enable our Ukrainian colleagues; both academics and practitioners, to begin to move forwards in integrating practice competence with academic achievement in a more systematic and structured manner.

We initially approached our first visit to Ukraine with excitement and apprehension. As stated earlier, we were firm in our commitment to social work values and adult learning principles. However, we were mindful of the fact that these values and principles may not have transferred across cultures. We were pleasantly surprised and pleased as we identified common ground in values and learning principles, and parallel processes relating these to practice teaching and learning. Our social work values, underpinned by CCETSW (1996), IFSW (2004), BASW (2004) and NOPT (2000), were resonant with our learners' identified values and principles. This was again confirmed when the authors undertook a similar teaching visit to Baku in Azerbaijan in August 2004. The same teaching techniques and methods were successfully employed within the same values framework. Our learners from across Azerbaijan received our input with the same enthusiasm as had our Ukrainian colleagues.

Given the differences in our three cultures, our experiences and research have underpinned our hypothesis that there is indeed a universality of values and educational principles that may be applied to social work education.

We intend to test this out further in the future!

Acknowledgements

There are many in England and Ukraine who have supported our project in Ukraine – thank you all, we are sorry we cannot do so by name. However, there are few who we do particularly wish to identify.

We are firstly indebted to all our wonderful students from Chernihiv Law Institute who put up with us in 2000, and then returned in 2003 to take part in this research. We thank the staff in the social work department who supported us, our interpreters, Sasha and Tatanya, and the Director of Chernihiv Law Institute Vasil Kubrak, for his continuing support, hospitality and faith in us.

We acknowledge the continuing support of Anglia Polytechnic University for both the teaching and research aspects of our visits.

We thank those who sponsored us by providing many items for distribution in Ukraine. These included Crystal Palace F.C., Chrysalis TV, and Henry Watson's Pottery.

We pay tribute to our wives, Lorna Ambler and Penny Black, and our families for their help and tolerance.

Finally, we wish to thank and our coordinator, interpreter and fellow researcher Tatanya Tartachnyck, Lecturer and now acting Head of Social Work Studies at Chernihiv Law Institute. Without Tanya none of this would have been possible – 'dyakuyu'.

5

A feminist perspective on North American practice learning

Dorothy C. Miller

Introduction

The slogan 'think globally, act locally' is one that I take to heart. The world is smaller than ever, and the more we learn from each other the better place the world will be. It's important as well to be discussing values and ethics in cultural contexts. Too often we make assumptions based on cultural attitudes disguised as value-based ethics.

This chapter is about value-based ethics in social work based on a feminist perspective. I must caution that there is not just one feminist perspective, however, but many. The paper addresses social work values based on experience in the practice and teaching of social work and a long-term exposure to and study of women's issues, from academic and practice perspectives. The most recent practice perspective is from work as Director of the Center for Women at Case Western Reserve University in Cleveland, Ohio, USA.

Social work practice learning in the USA

In the United States, 'practice learning' is called 'field education.' I will use those terms interchangeably throughout this paper. Social work practice in the USA is divided into two areas. 'Micro' practice is direct work with clients (individuals, families and groups) with regard to their social and emotional issues. The work is sometimes referred to as 'clinical practice.' 'Macro' practice includes administration, community organization, and task-centered (rather than therapeutic) group work.

Stemming from Charity Organization Societies and Settlement Houses in the late 19th and early 20th century, social work as a profession grew rapidly. In 1898 the New York School of Philanthropy, later called the Columbia University School of Social Work, was established to provide graduate level professional education for social workers. In 1920, the Association of Training Schools of Professional Social Work was founded, and later renamed the Council on Social Work Education in 1952. This organization accredits all schools of social work in the United States and has been very powerful in creating uniformity among schools.

Schools and programs strive to make themselves unique by offering opportunities for specialization, but in fact the basic education received from school to school differs more by the insights of the professors than it does in the content provided. There are 163 accredited Masters Degree (MSW) Programs in Social Work and 439 Bachelors Degree (BSW) programs. BSW programs were established in the 1960s in response to a perceived need for more trained social workers.

The National Association of Social Workers is the social work professional organization. Membership is voluntary, although most social work practitioners belong. States issue licenses for social workers to practice under the title of 'social worker.' NASW members who violate its code of ethics may be sanctioned by the organization but this is not related to licensure. However, the code is taught and used by schools to inculcate social work values.

Most USA social work practice takes place in government-run agencies and private, non-profit voluntary agencies. Social workers also find jobs in private, profit-making organizations that serve clients through corporate arrangements or client fees. Many social workers go into 'private practice' as therapists and receive fees either from clients' insurance or directly. Meanwhile, social work in the United States remains the 'stepchild' of the professions, undervalued. This is because we work disproportionately with the poor and because so many people working on the front lines are not 'professionally trained.' That is, they may be called 'social service workers' or other names and have not received degrees in social work from accredited institutions. There is also the issue of 'what is a profession?'

In 1915, the social scientist Abraham Flexner delivered a speech, 'Is Social Work a Profession?' at the National Conference on Social Welfare. He concluded that it was not. This talk remained famous for a long time because it identified a major struggle in the profession, one that in some ways goes on to this day. To make up for this undervaluing, our schools and our accrediting agency tend to be super-professional, precise, guarding the gates into and out of the schools, with regard to students and professors alike. This isn't in itself a bad thing, but sometimes results in rigidity and bureaucratic resistance to change. On the other hand, social work agencies and government entities have increased in their understanding of and trust in social work practice.

Cultural differences

It is a rather humbling experience at this point in history to be discussing American culture. What citizen of the world does not have an opinion about it and indeed, pretty good knowledge of it? But I will talk about how I think our particular culture affects our social work practice, practice teaching, and views.

Americans tend to be individualistic, value capitalist, market-driven solutions to social problems, and lack confidence or belief in an inherent 'work ethic' in other cultures and in Americans who are poor. We tend to value the nuclear family – that is husband-wife family much more than the 'extended' family of spread-out cousins, not to mention many generations. We 'say' we cherish children, but we bear minimal collective responsibility for them compared with the rest of the world.

The United States is the only developed country in the world that does not have a system of national health care. Neither do we have children's allowances. The numbers of those without health insurance grew from 41.2 million in 2001 to 45 million in 2003, the highest number on record.[1] This number does not include those people who are enrolled in various means-tested government-provided health insurance programs for certain categories of the poor. These insure less than half of the population. Substantial racial and ethnic disparities exist in health insurance coverage. In 2002, some 10 percent of white, non-Hispanic Americans were uninsured, compared to 20 percent of African-Americans, 18 percent of Asians and 32 percent of Latinos. The risk of being uninsured is particularly high for immigrants who are not citizens: 43 percent of non-citizens were uninsured. Given this information, it isn't surprising that the USA ranks 23rd out of 29 industrialized countries in infant mortality. As expected these mortality rates are primarily affected by rates among our poor and ethnic minority citizens and non-citizens. Many Americans are proud of saying that we have the best health care in the world. This could be true, but the health care we dispense doesn't go to everyone. Many people receive inferior care and then only in emergencies. People with good jobs and people who can afford it get good health care.

Majority Americans distrust strangers and are not very hospitable to those we don't know. We celebrate immigrants in inverse proportion to the time they have spent in this country and to the degree that they are 'grateful' for the opportunity to assimilate as much as possible. We believe that people who arrive on our shores should adhere to American white upper-class Christian notions of behavior and motivations behind that behavior. They should also speak English. Since these seem so obvious and easy, we usually assume that someone who doesn't adhere to them is deviant. There is also an increasing pressure to be overtly Christian and conservatively religious.

Of course the United States is multicultural. We still have large numbers of people who are 'newcomers' to the country, whose native language is not English, who do not speak English. Many descendants of Europeans, Asians, and South Americans continue to honor cultural and religious traditions that are different from, and sometimes contradictory to, broad-based American values. And most of the time, most of us get along pretty well. Some observers believe that class differences more than racial, ethnic and religious differences divide USA citizens from each other. Americans, like most people in the world, have double standards with regard to class. Today our magazines feature laudatory articles about women in professional jobs leaving work to be home with their children, while some of the same publications praise poor women, living in slum neighborhoods, for leaving their children in substandard day care to give their children an 'example' by trying to support them through dead-end jobs. Class consciousness often cuts across ethnic groups. Americans ignore or deny the problems that culture and class difference cause. Social workers, of course, are in the middle of them.

Problems with culture and ethics in social work practice

Mary Richmond's landmark book *Social Diagnosis*, published in 1917, taught social workers to focus on the 'person in situation,' setting out common principles for social workers to use in determining what clients need. One needed to 'start where the client is,' and consider the whole 'situation' (Richmond 1917). For a long time, these phrases have been spoken in social work practice teaching and they ring true. What complicates matters are questions about how to apply this simple advice. It is no longer evident where the client is, after all. And how do we define 'the situation.' In fact, our cultural attitudes affect how we interpret what the situation is and how we approach helping the client. Let me use practice with women and families as an example.

In the 1950s the cultural ideal for women was for them to be married with children and staying home to take care of those children. It was a white, middle-class cultural norm. Women in abusive relationships were advised to stay with their husbands and enter marital counselling with them, based on the belief that underlying problems in family dynamics caused the problem and each spouse needed to take equal responsibility for the battering. The popularity of family therapy grew at this time. It was only in the late 1960s that grass roots movements of women established shelters for battered women, places where women abused by their husbands could seek refuge for themselves and their children. They identified as patriarchal the view that physical harm that would otherwise be prosecuted if perpetrated on a stranger could be personal when it occurs between spouses. These shelters were run by volunteers at first, then paid staff, and were designed to 'empower' women before the term empowerment was introduced into social work jargon. The staff recognized that women who have been psychologically and physically battered need to take control over their lives. Shelter rules were developed with the participation of residents and residents were given the opportunity to make decisions for themselves whenever possible, within the parameters of group living.

Today, shelters are underfunded but have become professionalized and institutionalized, headed by professionally trained social workers. Women clients have less opportunity to participate in the shelter organization. Also, 'wife battering' is a term that is rarely used anymore. It has become 'domestic violence.' Of course, any institutional setting has to have rules, and shelters for abused women and children are no exception. These families are stressed and sometimes pathological. But the term 'domestic violence,' I suggest, even though it encompasses the real violence also done by women, tends to put distance between the perpetrator and the crime. In our cultural thinking we end up focusing entirely on the victim and not on the perpetrator. Consider the progression in our thinking:

John batters Jane.
Jane is battered by John.
Jane is battered.
Jane is a battered woman.
John has dropped out of the equation.

Culture has changed and continues to change our views of clients and their situations and so has professionalisation. 'Starting where the client is' means knowing what the client feels, what she wants, and how she interprets her situation. But there is always a social work interpretation. In the 1950s middle-class women dissatisfied with their roles as housewives were seen through a lens of psychoanalysis. These women were viewed as having conflicts with their femininity and their female roles. Today, many people would see these women's feelings as natural. Others would differentiate among women and see that some may be dissatisfied at home and others not. Fortunately, today, there is a strong emphasis on increasing women's 'empowerment,' building on women's strengths, and otherwise countering the older notion of women as helpless victims or persons who need protection, or the cause of all family problems.

Years ago, when I worked in New York City, I had an African American client who was having trouble with her teenage boy. The boy had spent some time in the south with his aunt and other relatives who helped to raise him. My supervisor suggested to me that the problem between mother and son was resentment on the part of the boy for his mother having sent him away for a time to be raised by others. I accepted that interpretation then, but today I think that we didn't take into account the fact that in African American communities, many people participate in a child's upbringing and that it isn't unusual for family to send a son or daughter to other family members for care. We didn't know much about this family's culture. Our interpretation influenced our judgment and my approach to the family's problems.

Our welfare programs for families began in 1935 but it was not until the 1960s that poor Black Americans were given their legal rights to be given aid. But the rules and regulations didn't work well for them. African Americans have a long tradition, that some historians have traced to Africa, of extended family relations, complex networks of people with blood ties and without blood ties living together or nearby and helping each other. Yet our welfare laws specifically designate nuclear families as recipients of aid and punish people who 'share' resources with so-called 'outsiders.' Even today we penalize two welfare-reliant women with children who live together, reducing their welfare payments. Faced with this cultural and policy infrastructure in which to work, social workers can become either punitive gatekeepers or co-conspirators with their law-breaking clients. Today the term 'cultural competency' has become part of the nomenclature of social work in the United States, and it part of our Code of Ethics. It's in the code as follows:

Cultural Competency and Social Diversity
(a) Social workers should understand culture and its function in human behavior and society, recognizing the strengths that exist in all cultures.
(b) Social workers should have a knowledge base of their clients' cultures and be able to demonstrate competence in the provision of services that are sensitive to clients' cultures and to differences among people and cultural groups.
(c) Social workers should obtain education about and seek to understand the nature of social diversity and oppression with respect to race, ethnicity, national origin, color, sex, sexual orientation, age, marital status, political belief, religion, and mental or physical disability.

But 'cultural competency' is not so easy. Cultures are complex and people within a culture differ enormously from each other. Within white Christianity, many of us accept and take for granted the many variations in cultural practices, but we tend to see 'other' cultures or religions as monolithic. Our social work textbooks do too. Although they recount the histories and cultural practices of cultures and enhance them with 'case histories,' they often only touch upon the variations that exist in life. Not all Jewish households 'keep kosher.' Not all Muslims strictly observe Ramadan.

We also face the problem of clashing with one's own culture. Today in the United States our welfare law demands that mothers applying for welfare go into the labor force as soon as work can be found. Our current standard is that all who have dependents must be breadwinners, except for the lucky women who happen to have husbands to support them and their children. If a woman wishes to be home with her children or rise above poverty, the best option, indeed the governmentally sanctioned option, is for her to marry and stay married.

Our policies make some implicit assumptions: that all people are heterosexual; that marriage is better than non-marital coupling or being single with children; that poverty should be a private matter between spouses. Furthermore, our policies imply that staying in a marriage, even if its an abusive or non-loving situation, is better than leaving it. We are spending millions of government dollars to encourage poor women to marry.

A single parent and her children have just 60 months over a lifetime (and in some states, less time) for the family to receive welfare maintenance payments. Eventually, labor force participation and/or marriage are a mother's only economic options. Many social workers have clients in this situation. One can say almost that both the client and the social worker are constrained by social polices and culture, regardless of what they believe would be the best solution for the family.

A social worker may think that a particular service, or educational opportunity, or special care for a child may be just the thing to recommend, but may know that there's no use in recommending it because such a pursuit is either against welfare rules or has the potential of making things worse for the family in the long run. Not recommending something beneficial may feel unethical. A family's lack of possibility may feel unethical. What is there to do when the cultural surroundings in themselves feel unethical?

Another governmental initiative in the USA today is the encouragement of what has been termed 'faith-based' services for people. Among private non-profit agencies, we have always had churches and other religious organizations providing services and many were government-subsidized. But usually they were not allowed to interject religious information and practice into their services and not allowed, when they received government funds, to discriminate against those from another religion. Today, the US Government is trying hard to promote these services and help them to include religious indoctrination and standards.

Faith-based agencies have often allowed religious beliefs to dictate their policies, in spite of laws to the contrary. Thus, teenage girls who are sexually active have often not been able to obtain birth control from Roman Catholic agencies, even though the girls were not Catholic. The Salvation Army in the United States operates many multi-service agencies throughout the country. They do not hire gay or lesbian workers. In their homeless shelters, they encourage husbands and wives to stay together but do not allow same-sex couples to do so. Today, the United States government applauds rather than prosecutes faith-based discrimination.

I suggest that many US social workers, no matter how 'culturally competent,' are forced every day to violate their professional code of ethics because of the nature of the agencies in which they work, the cultural beliefs that dictate the rules of the agency, and the 'situation' in which both the client and the worker find themselves.

Other social workers, including field supervisors and faculty, disagree with the code of ethics and agree with the majority culture. We don't know how this affects their practice and their teaching. In fact, the USA is in the middle of many culture wars. The President of the United States wants a constitutional amendment to ban gay marriage in a country that has popular TV shows featuring gay characters. Many heterosexual couples are living together and having children out of wedlock at a time when government policy is to promote only 'abstinence until marriage' to prevent teenage pregnancy. Moreover, people are choosing to form relationships that can be loosely termed 'families,' but are broader and different from those of our history.

University social work in a center for women

I work with students in an institution that ignores gender. 'Why isn't there a men's center?' is a frequent question. This attitude reminds me of Marshall McLuhan's well-known remark, 'I don't know who discovered water, but it was not a fish.' The most pressing issues for women on a college campus in the USA are sexual assault perpetrated by classmates, and disordered eating, accompanied by poor body image. Every day we see young women who are smart, articulate, poised, and seemingly confident. Then we find out that many of them hate themselves, think of themselves as fat and ugly. Although they are smart and accomplished, they are already planning their potential professional lives around future marriages. Many with 'disordered eating,' spend literally hours on treadmills trying to control themselves via exercise.

Other young women let it 'drop' in conversation that they've been sexually assaulted. In our culture, women have traditionally been blamed and blame themselves, for sexual assault. It would be wonderful to think that a new generation has a different attitude, and some do, but too much remains the same. Only today there is an additional cultural burden. Young women want to be popular and to be liked. They also have a kind of forthrightness that my generation didn't have. They want to have sexual agency – to control their own bodies and to assert their sexuality. They want to own and admit, in a way that my crowd didn't admit, their sexual desires and preferences. This is a good thing. But it also puts them into a different kind of danger – the danger of fooling themselves about what is going on when they are manipulated sexually.

Even as I describe my practice, I am making judgments. Students have been assaulted who don't always 'know' they have. How should we in the Center for Women proceed? It is essential to know these young women very well, listen hard, let them relate their experiences. We have to provide role models for them, reflecting in our own lives what can be possible for theirs. We have to be optimistic as well as realistic. One theoretician has identified what is called the 'carrier role' of social work, which 'entails transferring knowledge of various approaches to life from one group of people to another. She recommends looking to the 'wisdom of clients' as a source of 'practice enrichment' (Carroll, 1986). This is one description of what we strive to do in the Center.

Students in our school of social work at the university, who are required to secure some semblance of 'cultural competency,' nevertheless segregate themselves from each other racially and religiously. Aside from didactic learning situations, they do not take what they have learned outside of the classroom to form friendships with others who are different than themselves. I think that until and unless they do this, they are not going to do this in a practice situation. No matter how 'culturally competent' they are from book and classroom learning, they must listen to each other's stories informally, outside the classroom. The best way to be ethical and culturally savvy in a multicultural society is to immerse oneself in cultures that are not one's own.

Challenges and opportunities ahead

*   We have a *challenge* to be 'counter-cultural' and 'cultural' at the same time – working for social change and being 'in the moment' with clients who give us cultural explanations for their problems and students who only have their own culture as a frame of reference. No one can completely get 'outside' of one's culture. For example, I worry abut my weight and looks in a way that resembles the worries of our young students. I have to acknowledge this to myself and sometimes to them. At the same time, the social work task that presents itself is to apply a critical, counter-cultural analysis to the problem.
*   We are *challenged* to impart 'critical thinking' skills to social work students in practice learning situations – It is important for us all to question the assumptions we make in doing practice, and role model this questioning for social work students.
*   We are *challenged* and have the *opportunity*– to combine the best thinking of research, practice wisdom, theory, and cultural indicators

There are plusses and minuses within all of these areas. *Research* into methods of practice is important, measuring and evaluating what we do and how we do it. But we can't assume that all research is good and relevant. The fact is that many academics are doing research because their schools require it. Schools evaluate faculty not only by how much research they do, but by subject matter and the journals in which the research gets published. Some of the research can be relatively meaningless to the average practitioner. A colleague was recently denied tenure (lost her job) in a Social Work school because her published journal articles, geared toward practice, were not 'well placed.' Several articles were published in *Affilia: The Journal of Women and Social Work*, which has been publishing for about 30 years. Yet, even though it focuses on more than half the population and the majority of social workers, some scholars consider a journal about women too specialized and marginal.

In searching for good research, *'practice wisdom'* or the tacit knowledge that social workers 'on the ground' develop over the years, is an important source of knowledge. There is research indicating that tacit knowledge is applied quite thoughtfully and skillfully by social workers and is specific to the situation at hand (Zeira and Rosen, 2000). This is important to know, as such knowledge, based on experience, has often been dismissed out of hand because one couldn't prove that it works.

Moreover, we need *theory* in order to have necessary discussions of culture and ethics and how they inform practice. Here I'm speaking about philosophy and anthropology, theories about how and why we care for each other, and why we should. I think students should bring, and use, theoretical frameworks and questions to the practice setting. On the other hand, there are practice-related theories and models that can take on lives of their own. Psychoanalytic theory, for example, strangled the profession for quite a long time. Theoretical notions of practice swamp the social work journals. If we can remember that these theories are tools and not prescriptions, we can use them without using them to talk our concentration away from our clients.

- We are *challenged* to bridge the gap between professionally trained social workers and workers with 'on-the-job' training. I think the way to do this is to have a practical notion of professionalization rather than an elitist one, to recognize and stress contributions rather than deficiencies, and to build various methods of education and training into social work agencies and organizations.
- We are *challenged* to ensure that compassion is part of everything we do regardless of cultural constraints. No practitioner is ever

going to know all there is to know about another culture. I think that cultural competency, which is a good think, has to be complemented by humble, compassionate inquiry and vigorous listening. 'Would I want this for my own child, my own family?' is a good place to start. Yes, we can't take all the children home with us and we have to see lots of horrible situations that we can't change, but we can refrain from imposing insane, bureaucratic abuse on people.

- We are *challenged* to work for social change – to be activists for adequate social provision, and to teach our students to do this too. Social justice matters.

We are turning into a multicultural world and multi-familial world. Supporting the way people are choosing to live surely is better than railing against it. USA critics against gay marriage point out that disasters have resulted in countries that allow it. That is, there is more out-of-wedlock coupling and parenting and a high divorce rate. Without going into all the good and bad reasons for these things, taken alone this does not equal disaster. Maybe people wish to live differently. Maybe the indicators of disaster should be the degree of health, happiness, economic security, and cultural progress. New ways of coming together and taking care of each other, learning from other cultures, can be exciting rather than frightening. No one is trying to prevent people from entering into traditional marriage and relationships.

The world as we know it is extremely stressful and fraught with lingering 'old problems' and complicated by new ones. For a long time, social workers will be needed to mop things up, that is, clean up the messes the rest of the world creates. If we can do this without making new problems, with a view to social justice and compassion, then we'll have fulfilled the promise of social work.

Note

1. Washington, DC, Center on Budget and Policy Priorities, (2004) 'Number of Americans without insurance reaches highest level on record'.

6

Working towards culturally sensitive ethical practice in a multicultural society

Zita Weber

In the last two decades, there has been a lot written about multiculturalism and professional practice (Diaz-Lazaro and Cohen, 2001; Dominelli, 1988; Ivey, 1987; Ivey, Ivey and Simek-Morgan, 1997; Johnson, 1989; Ivey, Pedersen and Ivey, 2001; Nguyen and Bowles, 1998; Pedersen, 2000; Sue and Sue, 1977; Sue and Sue, 2003; Thompson, 1997; Wohl, 1989). Many of us are challenged by cultural diversity daily. Of late, some literature has explored the heightened awareness of the importance of cultural considerations in practice and the realisation that culturally competent practice and ethical decision-making need close reflection (Goldberg, 2000; Ivey, Pedersen and Ivey, 2001; Pack-Brown, Whittington-Clark and Parker, 1998; Pack-Brown and Williams, 2000; Pack-Brown and Williams, 2003).

My own thinking has become sharper over time. Because I'd been a migrant child, I always believed I had some real understanding and a deep level of empathy for cultural differences and sensibilities. However, over the years, I've discovered how much I had to learn about the realities of working with cultural diversity.

Teaching social work students at both undergraduate and graduate levels in Australia, a country recognised as comprising many different languages, cultural traditions and ethnic origins, I'm confronted by cultural sensitivity and competence issues and the ever-present ethical issues and dilemmas.

Post modern influences

Working towards culturally sensitive ethical practice presupposes a post modern stance (Christopher, 1996; Sue et al., 1996), and a move away from epistemological assumptions that are not necessarily shared across cultures. Such a stance entertains the existence of multiple belief systems and multiple perspectives (Gonzalez, 1997; Highlen, 1996; Sue et al, 1996). For instance, culturally sensitive practice would accept the existence of multiple worldviews and reinforce the notion that such worldviews are neither 'good or bad' nor 'right or wrong'. The refutation of this 'either or' view endorses the validity of each worldview and reinforces cultural relativism by recognising that each culture and attendant worldview is unique and can only be understood in itself and not by reference to any other culture and attendant worldview. Socio-politically, this stance is important as it inherently recognises the unfairness of one group imposing its standards on another.

Postmodernism also would inform the practitioner working towards culturally sensitive ethical practice that language does not equal 'perception of reality'. Adopting a relational view of language allows the practitioner to look beyond the truths and realities of the dominant culture as enshrined in language, both oral and written. Language and conceptual constructions vary tremendously between cultures. The importance of sensitivity to language and the way in which it is used may be illustrated in the encounter where the practitioner is using language and formulating questions from their cultural perspective regarding mental health concerns and the client is viewing the concerns from their different worldview. Such a situation is exemplified by Tsui and Schultz (1985) who write,

> The therapist must explicitly educate the client about the purpose of questions regarding clinical history, previous treatment information, family background and psychosocial stressors. The linkage of these issues to their current symptoms is not clear to many Asian clients. Many Asian clients conceive of mental distress as the result of physiological disorder or character flaws. This issue must be dealt with sensitively before any sensible therapeutic work can be effected. (pp.567-568)

Similarly, it is important to take into consideration cultural nuances of nonverbal cues as different cultural groups ascribe varied meaning to certain nonverbal behaviour. Eye contact, for instance, is expected among persons communicating in mainstream English-speaking cultures (Australia, Britain, USA, Canada). Certain stereotypes have developed regarding evasiveness and untrustworthiness of those people who avoid direct gazing. However, it is now well known that in some cultures, direct eye contact is regarded as disrespectful and an invasion of privacy. I experienced this cultural nuance when teaching in Texas where some Mexican-American students employed minimal eye contact with me. When I enquired about this, it was explained that as a older person in position of authority, it would be disrespectful to look me directly in the eye.

Failing to understand the significance of nonverbal behaviour may pose barriers to effective communication. Again, I experienced a cultural nuance in expectation when working with an Asian family. Whilst they expected me to provide advice as the 'authority' in the matter, I expected them to be more talkative and active in exploring options in the care of a member of the family who had been diagnosed with a major mental illness. Respect for authority may result in passivity and silence and as Tsui and Schultz (1985) note, 'Long gaps of silence may occur as the client waits patiently for the therapist to structure the interview, take charge and thus provide the solution' (p.565). Erroneously concluding that the client has flat affect or is unmotivated are potential hazards if the practitioner fails to correctly interpret the often smallest cultural nuance in nonverbal cues.

Although a post modern stance provides philosophical underpinnings that embrace the phenomena of cultural diversity and cultural sensitivity, translating concepts into dynamic, evolving practice poses some critical questions. Differences and nuances create challenges to our balancing of professional obligation with expectation of service delivery and determinations regarding the distinction between client behaviour that is culturally appropriate and behaviour that is problematic.

Some critical questions

How can we ensure that we develop and maintain cultural sensitivity? What of the danger of cultural encapsulation? Can we develop culturally sensitive ethical guidelines and bring culturally appropriate interpretations to our work? How do we go about teaching about values and ethics in a multicultural context? These are some questions that both students and practitioners ask at teaching and learning forums.

In one sense, the only way to address such questions is to pose further questions that challenge our ways of thinking. To avoid cultural encapsulation and a practice that is infused with Western assumptions and values we need to use all our critical reflective abilities to deconstruct the sometimes narrowly prescribed ways of working. We need to pose questions that challenge known practice around (i) not giving advice and suggestions because it may foster dependency (ii) not *taking* a teaching role (iii) not *accepting* gifts from clients and (iii) not *entering* into dual or multiple relationships because establishing boundaries is important (Sue et al, 1998).

What if the encounter with a client from a different culture demands that you exhibit the expertise and authority that otherwise would be discouraged as qualities that magnify power differentials between you and your client? What if the client's view about mental illness, for instance, is based on beliefs regarding magic and witchcraft, however, they ask that you educate them on terminology and the biomedical point of view, so that they might understand what is being communicated to them? What if the client proffers a small gift and presses you to accept at your last session together? What if …. There are endless 'what if…' questions we might pose to challenge our ways of thinking and ensure greater cultural sensitivity.

Essentially, these crucial questions point to the logic of returning to the fundamentals.

Whenever I pick up the Australian Association of Social Work (AASW) *Code of Ethics* (2000), I'm struck by two competing thoughts:

1. it is an essential resource – a valuable document;
2. it is a prescriptive document that has little interpretive value and if followed to the letter, one would be unable to practice.

There is the ambivalence of feeling contented that I have a reference book and the frustration that I'm told so little when it comes to sticky situations.

This Code, along with the British, U.S. and Canadian codes, is necessarily a broad-based document which can offer guidance, but cannot and should not be relied upon to solve ethical dilemmas involving cultural issues.

These codes contain concepts and ideas that are well-known among helping professionals. Nevertheless, when considering culturally sensitive and ethical practice, one crucial question arises: How can abstractions within codes be interpreted? Subsequent key questions could be: What questions should we be critically reflecting upon to become aware of the power of cultural variables? Most importantly, how can we translate this awareness into behaviour leading to effective intervention?

I intend to work towards developing culturally sensitive ethical practice guidelines within the context of a multicultural society by firstly, assessing the cultural sensitivity of the ethics codes and secondly, balancing culture and ethical codes.

Assessing cultural sensitivity of the ethics code

Professionals are expected to know and adhere to their ethics code. However, practitioners also need to demonstrate knowledge about their codes' sensitivity to diverse cultures. While codes have embedded within them requirements for cultural competence (for instance, in the AASW's *Code of Ethics* (2000) Section 4.2.4 is titled Cultural Awareness) how do some other principles fit with this?

For example, how do some cultural assumptions and expectations of our clients fit with ethics codes' statements regarding 'professional integrity'?

In the AASW *Code of Ethics*, Section 4.1.4 titled 'Professional Integrity' under (e) states: 'Social workers will ensure that professional relationships are not exploited to gain personal, material or financial advantage'. This sounds perfectly reasonable. But how does the practice of gift-giving to show appreciation to a practitioner fit with the principle of professional integrity as stated? There have been numerous occasions in my practice as a social worker when ethnic families have brought gifts to the final session. Does acceptance of such gifts, offered in the spirit of genuine appreciation, constitute some exploitative material gain? One supervisor had cautioned me about never accepting any gifts, taking an unqualified position. Another equally experienced supervisor had taken a much more relational position. Accepting the offered gift, in his view, turned on the 'it depends' argument. Cultural considerations might well be a dependent variable. Does accepting the gift suggest greater cultural sensitivity but less ethical practice or does rejecting the gift signify less sensitivity and greater adherence to ethical practice? Does a simplistic position of following the code to the letter make for good practice – culturally or otherwise? Perhaps the supervisor who recommended a 'it depends' position was suggesting a more balanced and measured approach, whereby cultural sensitivity was balanced with the spirit of, rather than the bald words, within a code of ethics.

Section 4.1.4 'Professional Integrity' includes under (g) cautions about dual relationships. Similar provisions appear in the BASW Code p. 7 under 3.4 'Integrity' 3.4.2 e 'To set and enforce explicit and appropriate professional boundaries to minimize the risk of conflict, exploitation or harm in all relationships with current or former service users, research participants, students, supervisees or colleagues.'

Both these codes of ethics add a qualification to this statement which, in effect, softens the statement. This qualification relates to minimising the 'risk of conflict, exploitation or harm'. In the BASW Code p. 7 under 3.4.2.f states 'To avoid any behaviour which may violate professional boundaries, result in unintentional harm or damage the professional relationship.'

This qualification is important and in order to understand what professional integrity might look like in relation to cultural sensitivity, it is worthwhile considering a relatively familiar scenario for many practitioners.

Let's take as an illustration the example of an invitation extended to you by a client to attend a social event. This invitation may come unexpectedly from a client or family you have been seeing for some time. The client may be from an ethnic background which has a collectivistic culture and she thinks of you, as her social worker, as 'family'. She asks that you attend her granddaughter's christening celebration. She would be 'honoured' if you did so.

This invitation poses a dilemma for you as you consider a response that, on the one hand, conforms to ethical sanctions against dual relationships and, on the other, respects the client's genuine valuing of you within the context of her culture. In previous sessions, she has explained that her cultural context embraces multiplicity in relationship roles and that she has had her priest and her doctor to dinner. For this client, the notion of strict professional boundaries is not part of her culture.

The questions that might crowd your mind could be:

- Is there a real risk of harm or exploitation if I attend the social event?
- Do I risk harming the client/s if I attend?
- What decision, attending or not attending, would best respect the client's dignity?
- How can I respond in a way that reflects the client's worth as an individual ?
  (questions adapted from Pack-Brown and Williams, 2003)

Also crowding your mind might be ethical decision-making frameworks to assist in working through dilemmas. One such model, forwarded by Welfel (1998) proposes an ethical decision-making model that consists of nine steps:

1. develop ethical sensitivity
2. define dilemma and options
3. refer to professional standards
4. search out ethics scholarship
5. apply ethical principles to the situation
6. consult with supervisor or respected colleagues
7. deliberate and decide
8. inform supervisor, implement and document actions
9. reflect on the experience

Such a model encourages the sort of critical questioning and reflection that offers the comfort of systemic analysis yet pushes the practitioner to consider the dilemma from several different perspectives (codes, scholarship and colleagues' views). Searching out ethics scholarship in this instance, would necessitate attention to diversity and difference and presuppose cultural sensitivity.

This framework implies balancing ethical considerations and for me, effective practice must have a balance.

Balancing culture and ethical codes

In this case of the invitation to a social event, an infant's christening, several responses are possible, not all of which are sensitive to both the client's culture and ethical principles. What are some of the options? What are their strengths and drawbacks?

Response 1

Explain to the client that your professional ethics code does not permit your participation in her social event. This is an example of a response emanating from a procedural perspective without consideration of the client's cultural context and practices. It would be fair to say that this response is not a culturally sensitive one. In fact, the client might be within her rights to beg the question, Who is protected here? The practitioner? The client? Both?

Response 2

Engage the client in discussion around the importance to her for you to attend. It might be argued that this response is more culturally sensitive than the first, however, it inherently questions the client's motives, suggesting to her that her request needs examination.

Response 3

Discuss with the client how she would feel if you did or did not attend. This response is similar to Response 2, suggesting that her request must be analysed. In addition, exploring her reactions to your options is premature and likely to confuse the client.

Response 4

Immediately accept the client's invitation to attend because you believe not doing so would offend the client and risk the professional relationship, which has been a long and positive one. This response, of immediate acceptance, might suggest that the practitioner has not carefully weighed the costs and benefits of agreeing to attend.

Response 5

Explain your dilemma to the client and tell her you wish to consult with colleagues, including someone from her ethnic background before you make a decision. In doing so, the practitioner positions the dilemma as one related to ethical constraints rather than to the client's request. This response considers the process of weighing cultural factors against ethical constraints. Nevertheless, by suggesting a consultation with an 'ethnic expert', the practitioner inherently questions the client's knowledge and understanding of what is appropriate.

Response 6

Share with the client that you feel honoured to be asked to such an important event in her life, but that her invitation presents a dilemma for you. This might be seen as a culturally sensitive statement because it positions the problem squarely in the practitioner's hands and shares the dilemma with the client, without demonstrating disrespect for the client's wisdom. This response might be followed by Response 3.

In my practice, I have known professionals from many varied backgrounds to take very different positions on invitations to social events, particularly when the request has come from a client from a different cultural background. I have never seen any of them take the decision lightly and certainly, when I decided to not attend my client's granddaughter's christening, I deliberated carefully, sought my supervisor's opinion and spoke with colleagues before deciding that although there was very little risk of real harm to the client in my attending the event, doing so would extend boundaries beyond their professional perimeters. My discussion with the client acknowledged the importance culturally for her inclusion of me in such an event and my respect for her cultural position. However, our discussion also covered respect for different positions and the need for us to continue in roles that clearly indicated that our relationship was professional rather than friendly. Nevertheless, I have known other practitioners who have attended social events and argued that their need to be culturally sensitive was greater than their need to maintain clear professional role identity.

There are many other examples of the need to balance culture and ethical codes. Notions related to client welfare is one.

In the AASW code, Section 3.1 Value: Human Dignity and Worth states that the social work profession holds that 'each person has a right to well-being, self-fulfilment and self-determination, consistent with the rights of others'. The American National Association of Social Workers (NASW) code contains an ethical principle valuing the 'inherent dignity and worth of the person.' Consistent with this value, social workers are required to 'treat each person in a caring and respectful fashion, (being) mindful of individual differences and cultural and ethnic diversity.' There is a similar provision in the BASW Code 3.1.2b p.4

Certainly, the overarching principle contained in these sections of various codes is protection of the welfare, or best interest, of the client. Nevertheless, these statements are broad and they leave room for interpretation and possibly, misinterpretation.

These codes, based as they are on principles of self-determination, individualism and clear relational boundaries, may well advocate a stance which is at odds with more interdependent, self-in-relation patterns of some ethnic and cultural ways of being. These contradictions may place practitioners in a bind – doing what is in the best interest of the client may conflict with various ethical codes. For instance, an Aboriginal woman with terminal cervical cancer rejected all forms of Western treatment in a large Sydney hospital and although not considered to be in her 'best interests' she insisted on discharging herself and going 'home' to her country community to be cared for by her extended family. For this Aboriginal woman, her self-determination could be seen to run counter to her best interests. However, she felt alienated in a big city hospital away from her family and her wish of 'going home' to be 'with family' was granted. In this case, the social worker and the team balanced ethical codes with culture and believed that the client would fare better in what she considered her own caring environment. The abstraction of 'best interests' needs careful consideration in such a case and self-determination regarding continuation or not of treatment viewed from different perspectives. Client welfare is not an obvious matter. Paradoxically, what appears to not be in the 'best interests' of the client, might in reality, be her 'best interests'.

Consider another situation. Clients from collectivist cultures for whom self-identity is inseparable from kinship systems may wish to bring family members with them to group therapy sessions. This may pose a problem for the professional in terms of the importance of maintaining the confidentiality of group members, yet the professional might understand that it is within the 'best interests' of the client to have the support they want. In this case, the professional must balance the rights of others and confidentiality with the expectation of different cultural groups and aim to negotiate a culturally sensitive decision. This notion of collectivity and support from family is raised by Pedersen (2000) who considers the concept of dependency as a potential source of conflict between ethical codes and culture.

In many diverse cultures, dependency on others is a way of life. Over time, cultural expectations regarding strong networks of interdependence have developed. Sometimes, socio-economic reasons have dictated that such interdependence is critical to the survival of many immigrants as well as indigenous people. Again a point of tension arises in that the ethics codes advise against relationships in which clients feel dependent on the professional. Perhaps several questions need to be asked to tease out the elements of the dilemma. Is it possible that a dependent relationship might be in the client's 'best interest' at least temporarily? Is it conceivable that a strong relationship with a professional might provide a sense of security and help the client, who feels they have little personal power, to build greater self-sufficiency? Again, paradoxically, the culturally sensitive practitioner might well be seen to be 'encouraging' dependency in order to help the client become more empowered eventually. Such tensions between individualism and collectivism and empowerment and dependency are common in work with people from diverse cultures and the ethical dilemmas they raise need careful reflection and logical consideration. A mere wish by the professional to be 'politically correct' is not enough, indeed, it runs counter to true professionalism, which requires that the professional be in a position to state clearly their dilemma and the reasons for their decision.

A cautionary note

There may be occasions when responding in a culturally sensitive manner may mean taking an historical view and working with its implications for clients in the contemporary context. For instance, an important consequence of oppression of indigenous and minority groups is the development of an intergenerational healthy cultural paranoia phenomenon (Ho, 1992; Paniagua, 1994; Smith, 1981). Amongst Australian Aboriginal people, for example, there is strong suspicion of professionals in official roles, particularly in relation to child welfare. Historically, welfare authorities routinely removed children from parents, a practice that has led to what is now known as 'the lost generations'. It makes perfect sense then, that Aboriginal people today might be distrustful of professionals who offer help, but are also in a position to recommend removal of children from families. Similarly, in the United States, this healthy paranoia phenomenon is evident amongst some African-American people who find it difficult to trust professionals who have disempowered them in the past (Smith, 1981).

However, the question might have to be asked: How do I determine the difference between client behaviour that is culturally appropriate and behaviour that is problematic? For instance, when does the healthy cultural paranoia exhibited by some oppressed cultural groups become problematic for them? Making that determination from a culturally sensitive stance is the challenge.

Some concluding thoughts

Neither cultural encapsulation where the professional is trapped in one way of thinking and believing that theirs is the universal way, nor a keen sense of political correctness makes for culturally sensitive practice. The professional who wishes to be culturally sensitive and competent and have confidence in making culturally sensitive ethical decisions, needs to live with uncertainty and acknowledge the power of the postmodernist stance regarding the existence, and legitimacy of, multiple worldviews. At all times, such a practitioner is performing a delicate balancing act. They must be guided by and bring together into a coherent whole, ethical decision-making frameworks, what the ethics codes state, what the client says and believes and what the practitioner believes reflects a sincere practice, faithful to the spirit, if not the letter, of the code of ethics.

7
The changing face of practice learning: A Chinese perspective

Diana Mak

Introduction

I had mixed feelings when approached last year to contribute a chapter on the topic of practice learning. I was anxious as to what to say as there has not been a lot of research effort on the theme, nonetheless, I was pleased to be asked as this offers an opportunity to articulate our efforts and experience during the past decade so that we can learn from an international audience. As an old Chinese saying goes

> Throw out a piece of brick in exchange for a piece of jade

Thus I shall be drawing on from the experiences, research and publications of the colleagues from the Department of Applied Social Sciences (APSS) of the Hong Kong Polytechnic University and I shall be approaching the topic in the following manner:

Part I   An overview of the Hong Kong context: post 1997 Hong Kong, social welfare and social work education with special reference to practice teaching in Hong Kong and the Mainland.

Part II   A discussion of one major core theme of the Chinese culture and the emerging issues in terms of the role of practice teaching.

Part III   The way ahead

Social work is an evolving profession that aims to improve the well being of the people in interaction with their environments based on the knowledge generated from theory/practice integration. However, the uncritical acceptance of knowledge so generated as objective, true and reliable has undergone much challenge during the past two decades (Yuen, 2001, 2003, 2004; Boud and Miller, 1996). Further, it has been pointed out by scholars of the west that much of these theories has come from western developed countries which have not considered local cultures, and distorted the interpretations of local needs (Midgley, 1981) In Hong Kong, where over 99% of the population is Chinese, we encounter both of the above issues simultaneously, so that an ongoing critical reflection on the theory/practice integration process becomes critical for the development of appropriate knowledge to meet local needs. How do we, then, ensure that our social work curricula take this into account, and then develop the students' ability in critical thinking in their attempts to integrate theory/ practice?

In this chapter, I would like to present an initial discussion on the experience of a group of Hong Kong academics in addressing the above issue, but before venturing into the discussion, I shall give a brief overview of the post 1997 Hong Kong context: social welfare and social work education situation. In view of the time constraint, I shall focus on one major core theme of the Chinese culture and its related issues that impact on social work practice, teaching/learning, followed by a brief discussion on the responses made by a group of academics, leading to suggestions on the way ahead.

Part I: Overview of Hong Kong

Hong Kong is located in the south-east of China, serving as the southern gate of China to the rest of the world.

Hong Kong, its people, its way of life, and its institutions are consequences shaped by the interacting forces of our colonial past and our historical links with the Mainland. This is the eighth year since our return to the People's Republic of China (PRC). This move to our socialist motherland has not changed the nature of Hong Kong as it is run on an outright capitalistic system with the government holding onto a free economy doctrine, formulating policies that favour the business sector and the rich. Meanwhile, China's entry into the World Trade Organization has brought both opportunities and fierce competition for Hong Kong. These years have been by no means uneventful and the Hong Kong people experience its frustrations and uncertainties: there is increased competition for capital and labour, some of these arose from the rapid development of major mainland Chinese cities like Guangzhou and Shanghai; locally, we had to cope with the collapse of the property market, followed by consecutive years of economic decline and deflation leading to a burgeoning structural budget deficit; unemployment stood at about 6%; we also faced an increasingly aged and more dependent population with a large pool of locally educated and low-skill workers. A close look at the data reflecting the welfare scene depicts social problems on the rise (Appendix 1).

This has been complicated by the 'new arrivals' from the Mainland. According to government statistics, in 2001, those who have resided in Hong Kong for less than seven years constitute 4% of Hong Kong's total population, an increase of 50% in ten years. Although Hong Kong has been built by periodic flows of mainlanders' resources and efforts; in times of weak economy, 'immigrants' seeking refuge in Hong Kong pose as threats. This, unfortunately, has been further compounded by the people's low trust in the HKSAR's competence to address the critical situation in Hong Kong.

In face of the situation, the top priority of the Government was to restore the budget balance. A wholesale reduction in Government expenditure has been pursued. Government activities are seen as a burden to the dwindling economy and a major disadvantage to competition with other cities in the region. The Government has adopted a 'small government' policy by which it withdraws its 'rowing' role, shifting the provision of public services to the non-governmental sector. It undertook reform on the subvention system that has supported the social welfare programmes provided by the non-governmental sector (which constituted over 80%) for several decades and changed the funding of the non-governmental organization (NGO) projects to lump sum grants; while this has given apparent flexibility to agency administrators, it has also sharpened competition among agencies to bid for services at a low cost. In the process, it has been observed that the unit cost of some of the services had been suppressed in order to win the competitive bid. To ensure value for money, the agencies are held accountable for the quality of service through funding contracts, service agreements, performance standards, and various managerial measures. Such escalating pressure for higher accountability and the need to demonstrate quality performance in terms of cost effectiveness and efficiency apply to both the non-governmental as well as the governmental sectors. The culture of managerialism has begun.

In such a context, public expenditure in heath and welfare programmes are seen as detrimental to the society's weak economy. Health and welfare policies reveal an even more remedial approach: the definition of needs became more specific to rationalize the allocation of reduced societal resources to meet such needs. The Comprehensive Social Security Assistance (CSSA), a public assistance scheme, is seen as creating a dependency culture among the poor; a 'workfare' approach was adopted and self-reliance has been emphasized. Reviews in health care reforms led to increased fees charged on medical consultations, prescriptions, etc. Such moves have caused much anguish to the poor and probably delay their access to necessary services. Where identified need falls beyond the restrictive definition, the private, non-governmental or philanthropic organizations will come in to meet the gap. Simultaneously, volunteerism has been actively promoted to support inadequate resources to meet needs. Volunteerism, a worthwhile activity, cannot really replace professional service.

A factor that directly affects social work education and hence practice teaching/learning in social work is the reform in education. An overhaul of the secondary and post-secondary education system has been underway..One of the specific results that impacts social work education is the anticipated withdrawal of the Government subsidy from the sub-degrees which produces the first level formally qualified social workers in Hong Kong. The direction seems to be that Government would only subsidized the first degree programmes. Evidently this will upgrade the qualification of the social work workforce, however, individual university's possible withdrawal of funding support to part-timers who rely on in-service training to upgrade themselves will result in their being sandwiched between a reduction in salary as well as a rapid increase in tuition fees!

In view of the weak economy, the central government of the People's Republic of China has recently introduced a number of policies to stimulate the economic growth of Hong Kong, and as a result, there are signs pointing to a stronger economic recovery; nevertheless, in the dominant view of the decision makers, health and welfare are basically the individual and the family's responsibility, and this will impact on the allocation of resources that determine the related policy background in the changing Hong Kong, let us take a brief overview of the social work education in Hong Kong and the Mainland.

Social work education in Hong Kong

The training and education of social workers in Hong Kong refers to the pre-qualification and in-service training programmes. The following six training institution offer programmes of both natures.

- Chinese University of Hong Kong (CUHK)
- City University of Hong Kong (CityU HK)
- Hong Kong Baptist University (HKBU)
- Hong Kong Polytechnic University (HK PolyU)
- University of Hong Kong (HKU)
- Hong Kong Shue Yan College (HKSYC – a private College)

Graduates of their qualifying programmes can register as Registered Social Workers at the Social Workers Registration Board (SWRB). The Social Welfare Department (SWD), the Hong Kong Council of Social Service (HKCSS – a Council of over 200 non-governmental organizations), individual non-governmental organizations and the Hong Kong Social Workers Association (HKSWA) share the mission of providing in-service training for social workers.

The local training institutions provide qualifying social work programmes of the following types:

- Sub-degree level training producing graduates of the Higher diploma in Social Work / Associate of Social Science in social work.
- Baccalaureates level education awarding graduates with titles such as Bachelor of Social Work, Bachelor of Social Science with major in Social Work or Bachelor of Arts (Hons) in Social Work.
- Post-graduate level education awarding Master of Social Work / Master of Social Sciences. This includes two levels of training programmes: the more advanced level building on the baccalaureates level and the pre-qualification level for those who join with a non-social work first degree.

All first-level training adopts a generalist approach, aiming to equip social workers to perform a wide range of tasks including direct service delivery, service planning, management, research, policy analysis in a variety of settings serving different target groups. To enable graduates to be registered as social workers with the SWRB, the curricula must encompass the following core subject areas:

- human behaviour and social environment;
- social welfare system and social policies;
- social work practice and theories;
- social sciences / liberal arts knowledge; and
- field practicum (minimum 800 hours for degree programmes and 700 hours for the non-degree programmes)

A majority of these training opportunities are full-time, while part-time programmes are offered for those who are already serving in the welfare field.

Although all these qualifying programmes aim to produce competent social work graduates, a recent review shows that different training institutions may embrace different scholastic orientations and focus (Advisory Committee on Social Work Training and Manpower Planning, Draft 1, October 2003)[*1].

Field practicums are resourced by Government funds as part of the lump sum grant allocated to Universities through the University Grants Committee. These are structured into concurrent (two days per week) and block placements (five days per week) where students provide real life service to service users. These all take place in a wide range of settings, in the public and non-profit making organizations (which include the non-governmental welfare organizations).

The selection of placements, matching, monitoring quality assurance and the coordination of practicum teaching are normally the responsibility of the academic colleagues in the universities. To date, basically two different models are adopted, namely: 'a long-arm model', where hourly paid/sessional practicum teachers are employed as fieldwork supervisors (practice teachers) for the students, leaving the coordination and theory/practice integration to the academic colleagues in the training institutions. Staff of the organizations offering placements often serve as practice teachers; a second model termed 'an integrated model' is to employ part-time contract staff, monthly paid on an appropriate salary scale, as practicum teachers, supervising students placed in the field. Incidentally, full time colleagues in social work also teach a very small number of students in practicum so as to be abreast with the changes in the welfare field. These practicum teachers, being full time and part-time colleagues of the University, and familiar with the curriculum, are expected to optimize the process of integrating theory/practice with the students.

Each model has its strengths and drawbacks (as this is not the focus of this paper, we shall not further discuss them here). The department which I come from, The Departmental of Applied Social Sciences (APSS), has adopted the integrated model during the past decade, however, with the drastic reduction of funds, how to sustain or modify the model so as to retain the positive features and the quality of practicum teaching/learning will be an issue of concern.

Social work education in the Chinese Mainland

Since the adoption of the economic reform and the opening up policy in 1979, the People Republic of China (PRC) has taken a more open attitude to its needs and problems. It was through a regional conference jointly organized by the Asian pacific Association of Social Work Education and the Peking University in December 1988 that the PRC was officially introduced to the social work profession in the international scene. At the close of the conference, four universities were mandated to run pilot training programmes for social workers. By the middle of 2003, about 125 universities/ colleges/institutes had launched social work programmes of various types in PRC, (and the numbers are on the increase!). However, with almost no qualified social work staff serving as teachers of these programmes, social work education in the Mainland is very much at an early stage.

In the year 2000, two attempts were made to address this issue:

1. The University of Hong Kong, Department of Social Work and Administration, supported by the Fuen Dan University, Shanghai, launched a masters' programme to holders of baccalaureate degrees who are interested in social work. The programme was taught by qualified social work academics from Hong Kong and oversea universities. Practicum teaching took place in a number of welfare organizations in Shanghai.
2. Another attempt was a collaboration between APSS, the HK PolyU and the Department of Sociology of Peking University. The programme was taught at Masters' level aiming to train a core group of social work educators who could take up the future leadership in developing social work education on the Chinese Mainland (adopting a 'training of the trainers' approach). The Programme recruited trainees from all over the nation, the first cohort of students came from 11 social work training institutions and seven cities from various parts of PRC. Practicum teaching took place in Yunnan for rural social work, in Peking for urban social work, in Shanghai to work with young people with problems. Trainees would also spend a third practicum in Hong Kong. All practicum teaching (800 hrs) is supervised by Hong Kong qualified social work teachers. This programme produced its first graduates in 2003-04. Since the first inception date, APSS has developed 3 training centres in the PRC for practice teaching. Both the HKU and the HK PolyU programmes were validated, approved and recognized by the Ministry of Education, People's Republic of China.

The above is a very crude outline of social work education in the Hong Kong and Mainland China context.

Part II: Discussion on one major cultural theme: Familism

I shall focus on just one major theme, familism, which is considered the core culture in the traditional Chinese society, but before we begin, two points are worth noting:

1. Values in our core culture have been changing fast, especially so with the tremendous changes found in the social, economic, political aspects of Hong Kong and China during the last five decades.

2. While the theme is a common phenomenon for the people of Hong Kong and the Mainland, it manifests itself differently as the two places have gone through very different development: Hong Kong under the British rule and influence for over a hundred and forty years, hence a rather long exposure to western culture and values, while the Mainland has adopted a closed door policy since 1949. However, it initiated its economic reform and opening-up policy in 1979, and the changes have been rapid.

Familism and its value system

Familism or familial culture has been recognized as one major core cultural themes of the traditional Chinese society. Although much of our living today, in Hong Kong and the Mainland, differ from that of the traditional familism, its value system still have much influence on our thinking and behaviour. Familism can be understood at two levels:

- at a more concrete human relationship level *and*
- at more abstract or general level

At the more concrete level, familism provides principles and guide to human behaviour. In this familial culture, the most important relationship is 'kinship'. Fei (1992) compares this with the concentrated circles of throwing a stone into a lake. Like the ripples in the lake, social relationship in the Chinese society exhibits a self-centred quality, through marriage and giving birth to children, this can be extended to form a network of relationships with the self at the centre and include a large number of people of the past, present and the future. Although it is vast, each network is like a spider's web and each web has a 'self' as its centre; each is distinct, spreading out from the individual's personal connections. Such personal connections constitute a common system of notation which identifies how the individual is related to other individuals in a particular way. Thus the Chinese 'self' is a relational 'self', relating oneself to the network of social relationships, while in the west, the 'self' is perceived more as an isolated 'self', often perceived as an atomic individual.

In the west, all members in an organization are alike, enjoying the same entitlement to rights. In the Chinese pattern, this is different; each circle spread out from the centre (which the 'self' occupies) becomes more distant and less significant. This arrangement of the basic structure of the traditional Chinese society is what Fei (1992) calls 'a differential mode of association'. This basic characteristic of the Chinese social relationship is what Confucius called 'renlun' (human relationship). The essence lies in the 'five sets of human relationship: between sovereign and subject, father and son, husband and wife, among brothers and among friends'. The Book of Rites, 'li', one of the Confucian classics, contains the discussion of ritual practices that guides human behaviour. Confucius alleged that one should 'control oneself and conform to the rituals'; it is through practising such self-constraint that one will cultivate one's moral character.

Subduing the self to follow the rites is the most important feature and this is the starting point in the system of morality inherent in the Chinese social structure. The social networks, extended from the self, form the social spheres. Each of these social spheres is sustained by a specific type of social ethic: for example, the ethical values that match the relations between parents and children is filial piety, and those which concern the siblings born of the same parents is fraternal duty; the ethical values to guide friendship are loyalty and sincerity. This sustains human relationships and facilitates peace and harmony in the familial culture. Thus one who fails to perform according to expectations will 'lose face'.

Francis Hsu's concept of the 'father-son dyad' helps us to understand human relationship in the traditional Chinese society from another angle. In the traditional Chinese society, the 'father-son dyad' is at the centre of blood relationship and the blood relationship is extended upwards to our ancestral lineage and downwards to future generations. Such arrangement of familism contributes to the structure of a lineage. As the relationship is closer or the more distant, so a different extent of authority is exhibited, with the senior being superior and the junior inferior.

Members of the lineage are required to act according to the goal of continuing and expanding the lineage. Thus we can see that the familial culture revolves around the axis of the father-son dyad, and this features as an important characteristic of the patriarchal culture, giving rise to the male-female relationship, contributing to the 'men dominant, women subservient' attitude.

Yuen (1993) combines Hsu's 'father-son dyad' and Fei's 'differential mode of association' to further throw light on the behaviour of the Chinese. With the 'father-son dyad' as the vertical axis, placing the son at the centre point and Fei's 'differential mode of association' horizontally defines the relationships from the closest to the most distant kin, thus forming a network of human relationship. The intensity of affect and emotions thinning as the relationship extends horizontally outwards from the centre; Such defined relationships also serve the basis for the distribution of resources and benefits, including wealth.

Yuen, in comparing the differences between the Chinese and the Western conception of human relationships, opines that the Chinese, pivoting on the father-son dyad, 'emphasize the continuity of a relationship whereas the westerners emphasize on its function'. Following on from this 'continuity-based relationship', the underlying value system is a tendency to conform to group values, the bases for value judgement and distribution of benefits depending on the degree of relationship closeness as depicted in the 'differential mode of association'.

In contrast, the western value system, basing itself on a functional orientation in relationships, tends to regard the individual's self-interest as the important drive for one's behaviour and to adopt the principle of fairness as the criterion for the distribution of resources. These two value systems, as espoused by Yuen, will lead to different criteria for value judgement and orientation, which will give rise to different concepts of the self and lead to different modes of behaviour.

As the Chinese emphasize the well-being of the collectivity of the lineage, their self-concept cannot be distinguished from the concept of the 'larger self' which constraints personal likes and dislikes. However, their western counterparts tend to see individual self-interest as the principal guiding principle despite the influences exerted on them by the larger society. When the above is applied to family relationship and marriage matters, the patriarchal culture and the 'men decide, women follow' approach become a characteristic of familism.

The development of individual autonomy

Yuen (1998) conceives western individualism and describes it as

> a state or capacity for the self-initiation of thoughts and actions. People who are autonomous can make decisions about their actions on their own, free from external constraint ... [which he refers to mainly as the use of force] ... a second way is relating autonomy to 'internal constraint' ... a process of socialization and the social/moral norm is internalized as an individual's value orientation, forming part of that individual's character. '

Here, Yuen proceeds to examine the differences between traditional Chinese views and modern Western views on the notion of individual autonomy: Traditional Confucian thinking stresses the nurturing of the internal, transcendental individual autonomy and the followers of Confucius' view that the process of transcendence relies on the cultivation and nurturing of one's inner-self, emphasizing autonomy in the development of the moral sphere. In contrast, the Western notion of autonomy, despite some influence from the 'larger self' or significant others, stresses individual decision in the areas of material choices and personal desires.

From the above perspective, the Confucians would hold that social norms are developed from the individual subjective moral self and this can be extended outward from the individual to the family, to relatives and friends, guided by the rules of propriety or 'li'. Thus 'weaving together a social relations network based on family and lineage ties, sustains human relationships, facilitates peace and harmony in the familial culture', nonetheless, it does not necessarily ensure the development of individual autonomy of transcendence.

The above is a positive way of looking at the influence of the

Chinese family and lineage structure and Chinese culture. Less positively, the Confucian doctrine has been accused of stifling the development of individual autonomy, e.g. the five human relationships which have revolved round Hsu's 'father-son dyad', together with the attribute of 'authority', will lead to a compliance to one's senior, and such pattern can be transferred to the other social relationships.

While many of the above key features are being weakened, elements of them can be recognized and they still guide the behaviour of the Chinese to varying extents today.

At the more abstract level of familism, Hsu has identified four attributes in his 'father-son dyad' which are perceived to be rooted in the deep structure of the Chinese Culture. These are continuity, inclusiveness, authority and asexuality.

Hsu opines that a relationship based on the father-son relationship will naturally emphasize continuity. As the father-son blood relationships is stable and acts as the core, all other relationships, such as husband-wife, friendship, are subsumed under the attribute of continuity. When the father-son dyad is placed at the centre, the attribute of inclusiveness can be visualized. Depending on whether they are closer or more distant, relationships exhibit different extent of authority, with the senior being superior and the junior inferior; Since this perspective depicts the dominance of the father-son dyad and the male gender, husband-wife or gender relationships, the intrinsic gender differences are as a consequence, ignored. The above analysis helps to understand the deep structure of the traditional Chinese culture.

Examples from the social work practice

The following are examples from our practice illustrating traces of the elements of the core culture.

A social worker who, having built trusting relationship with a battered wife client, entered into deep conversation with her on her client's perception of the situation and her future. Although the marriage relationship had long been unsatisfactory and that she had been battered repeatedly by her husband, the client would not consider the option of divorce. Reasons could be many: the couple had children and the client wanted the family to remain intact;

there were cases where no children were involved but the battered wives still would not leave as they believe that they must be loyal to the marriage.

If one is married to a cock, one should follow the cock' way; when one is married to a dog, one then follows the dog's way.

If you choose to stay with your husband, how would you address the issues arising from the unsatisfactory relationship in the future?' 'Be patient, be tolerant and keep harmony in the family', replied the battered wife.

When the case was used in our seminar workshops, it was reported that similar attitudes were shared by our young students in their twenties!

One active elderly lady member of the social centre, was discovered by the social worker, to have been abused by her daughter-in-law, only after a few sessions of intensive interviews. The alleged reason for not disclosing her problem earlier was because one should not disclose one unpleasant events outside one's family. It is not proper to do so. '

A Chinese male adult may have much respect and affection for his mother, but when it comes to making important family decisions, he would expect that he will have the decision making power.

In community development projects, it is not unusual to find service users 'supporting' community action activities purely because they have a good relationship with the social worker, their 'support' is 'to give face' to the worker.

Social workers and medical personnel have found it difficult to successfully persuade the public to organ donation because it is a common belief that to preserve a complete dead body is important for the transformation of one's soul in the after-life.

Some of my practice teachers, when comparing the PRC trainees and the HK students, have found that the former were much more courteous and respectful for them as teachers, saying, 'Once a teacher, forever a teacher!'

When it came to discussing possible changes in the social system, they had found the PRC trainees much more cautious, relatively slow or even resistant in making slight changes as it seemed that challenging authority is not necessary.

The above examples show us that culture and values are so deeply rooted in our culture that they are very much embodied in our way of life. While modernisation and societal system take place and the traditional values may be weakened, traces and elements of culture and values can be easily detected. As social workers and social work teachers, we work and live with them every day.

Let us now turn to some of the issues and discuss how we have tried to cope with them. Please bear with me that my examples here will be mainly drawn from the work of my colleagues in APSS.

Issues and responses

Practice teacher/student relationship

This area has been well researched, and perhaps no one would disagree that the practice teacher/student relationship is the pivotal bond that facilitates student learning. M.S. Tsui made qualitative studies on the. supervisor-supervisee relationship in Hong Kong (2002, 2004). Although these studies are not strictly on practice teacher/student relationship, I find them relevant to our discussion. Tsui found that the supervisory relationship is a complicated mix of hierarchical, collegial and familial relationship. It is not only organizational and professional but also cultural and personal. Tsui found that in times of tension, supervisors relied quite a bit on 'qing, yuan and face'[2] to relieve the tension and to maintain harmony in their relationship with their supervisees. In so doing, the supervisors found that this has enhanced mutual tolerance, acceptance and respect for one another.

While such a finding enriches our understanding of the supervisor-supervisee relationship, it further complicates the supervisory process, because phenomena like this may be abused and used as a form of control over the private life of the supervisee or in the case of 'yuan', used as a reason to resist change! In both studies, Tsui repeatedly found that the supervisees would prefer supervisors of the same sex while the same preference was shown by the supervisors of their supervisees. This reminded me of Fei's study on the rural Chinese society in *The Foundations of Chinese Society* (1992), when he was discussing the attitude between men and women. On this, Fei stated,

The force that stablises social relationships is not emotion but understanding. Understanding means accepting a common frame of reference ..... In rural society, it is the differences in biology that prevent people who live closely together from obtaining a full understanding of each other .... The biological differences that eternally divide people are the sexual differences between men and women. No one has ever personally experienced what it is to be a member of the opposite sex .... In reality, everyone has .... felt a lack of mutual understanding between the sexes. '

Does this stimulate us to ask further questions on Tsui's findings?

Based on the above, Tsui advocates cultural sensitivity training for effective practice teaching.

Issue on authority

In his qualitative study (2004) exploring the supervisory relationship between social work supervisors and frontline social workers in Hong Kong, Tsui finds that the perception of a hierarchical relationship by the supervisees is obvious, and that compliance to authority is the norm in practice. Supervisors participating in the study tended to adopt a 'consensus by consultations and consent' approach. Although work on a comparable topic in the mainland has not yet been published, experience informs us that, compared with HK students, our Mainland trainees are relatively slow in taking up system change as an intervention strategy because it seems difficult for them to challenge authority.

Hong Kong practice teachers from their initial experience have found trainees from mainland China very respectful to their teachers. They are mindful of the outcomes more than the learning process. They are particularly sensitive to the status, rank and file as well as the power structure within the department. Practice teachers caution that manipulation of their relationship with the teaching staff for personal gain may take place. The practice teachers do find the teaching of the PRC trainees a challenge: they, coming from a culture with which the practice teachers are unfamiliar, tend to be cautious and reserved and take longer to enter into an open and trusting learning relationship with the practice teachers. Therefore, to develop the cultural sensitivity in the practice teachers would be critical in reaching these trainees from the mainland.

Managerialism and its impact on practice

In recent years, Hong Kong has seen welfare services become more commodified and welfare organizations, public and non-governmental organizations (NGOs), being hard-pressed by the introduction of manergerialism. NGOs and their social workers are expected to be accountable and output oriented, and to demonstrate value for money, cost-effectiveness and efficiency. With the budget reductions, agencies became very cooperative, and very cost conscious; a standard-based performance culture has emerged. Such a cultural shift enforces a superficial, fragmented and piece-meal approach to practice. It is non-conducive to the nurturing of the social work student in understanding the service user more holistically, and in the development of their commitment to serve.

If APSS is forced to change from 'the integrated model' to 'the long arm model', that is into adopting the model of purchasing practice teaching from the welfare organizations, the critical issue, then, will be how to ensure that the practice teachers (the organizations' hard pressed social workers) will be able to deliver quality teaching to our students during placement. How would APSS and the practice teachers convert the adverse conditions in the placement settings into a nurturing and positive learning environment for our students?

Issues faced by an emerging profession in the mainland

As social work is still an emerging profession in the Chinese Mainland, the lack of trained social work teachers and the location of appropriate practicum placements are very real difficulties under limited resources. Since we are in a 'take-off phase', such issues may be overcome by developing a critical mass to nurture exemplars as models for good practice.

The above are some of the issues we face in practicum teaching/ learning in Hong Kong and the Mainland. As the process of modernization and westernization have weakened our traditional culture and values, how then can we address these issues? The following are some suggestions:

Affirmation of the role and function of practice teaching/learning in the education of social workers

As practice teaching/learning integrates the practice and the academic learning, the teaching/learning process in the practice situation has become the text for both teacher and student. This constitutes the platform whereby assumptions, and values can be examined, theories derived from western context may be challenged and concepts can be re-defined. ; in other words, practice teaching breeds a rich learning ground and is therefore of paramount importance in the education of social workers. Such a stand needs to be clearly articulated in our social work education policy, reflected in our budget allocation, elaborated in our curricula and, in-built in staff development to ensure practice teaching/learning's role in the education of social workers.

Facilitating learners to be culturally sensitive

We need to be aware of the incompatibility of western theories when these are applied to the Chinese contexts:

K.S. Yip, in his academic exploration (2001) on the impact of the Chinese culture on social work practice, distinguishes 'indigenization' of social work knowledge with the authentisation approach. He defines the former as 'adapting western models and concepts to understand the different needs of the Chinese/ethnic group' while the latter refers to the identification, articulation and conceptualization of the Chinese/ethnic group's authentic wisdom and these are integrated into the process in working with the service users. If applied to the practice teaching situation, this demands that the teacher-student free themselves from the fetters of western knowledge, to involve themselves deeply with compassion, with the service user, in the here-and-now situation.

Yip, through his reflection on his ten year's collaboration with a non-governmental organization, also demonstrated how sensitivity in the Chinese culture had helped to build a natural locality based network project with the single and chronically ill elderly; in the process, he and his colleagues in the NGO helped the residents developed a mutual help network by using ideas and norms from the Chinese culture found in their daily experience.

M.S. Tsui works with a number of colleagues in the study of social work staff supervision and concludes that Chinese culture has much impact on the supervisory relationship and advocates that cultural sensitivity is crucial to cross-cultural supervision and effective supervisory practice.

The search for an alternative paradigm

Beyond being aware, we need to invest in the search for an alternative paradigm, with the aim of developing and building coherent theories from social science and social work knowledge that is of relevance to the Chinese context:

Over a period of fifteen years, S.P. Yuen and the philosophy team (1990-2004)[3], adopting the thick description research method, have developed an original theoretical framework which innovatively integrates the following elements:

- contemporary western social theory with particular reference to critical hermaneutics;
- Chinese cultural thought with special reference to Confucianism;
- social work theory and practice.

The framework has been used to study the changing conception of modern Chinese identity in the Chinese Mainland, Taiwan and Hong Kong, with particular reference to the problem of indigenization in social science and social work practice. Two books, both published in 2004, reflect this work: the English translation of *Marriage, Gender and Sex in a contemporary Chinese Village* (2004), and *Reconstitution of Social Work: Towards a hermeneutical conception of social work practice*, in Chinese (which is being translated into English at the time of writing).

It is noteworthy that S.P. Yuen has developed an approach to integrate core critical hermeneutical themes with Chinese culture as well as counseling practice in social work. He and his team have proposed that a strong value involvement of the social work practitioner is necessary; the practitioner, with deep empathetic understanding, carefully listens to the narration of the service user, engages in a critical dialogical discourse with him/her. Together, a process will evolve whereby the practitioner-service user dyad will construct the problem, discuss the options and the meanings,benefits and disadvantages involved before making a decision on how to address the problem. In the process, both practitioner and service user will need to articulate and examine the beliefs, values, assumptions, tacit knowledge behind the views suggested; in other words, the practitioner and service user will enter into a open, deep conversation which would involve in the making of moral judgements. Thus, Yuen and team advocate social work as moral practice.

Staff development

The above issues all point to the need for continuous development for the practitioner as well as practice teachers as cultural sensitive professionals. The University can serve as a vehicle whereby staff development sessions/courses may be organized to raise the practice teachers' capacity to address the issues, paradoxes, and dilemmas daily encountered at work. Such sessions will provide collegial support to question existing grounds, to explore new fronts, to re-define relationships with self, others and the world. At this moment in time, the huge demand and pressure of workload and responsibilities on the practitioner, as a consequence of the introduction of a multitude of managerial measures have made the practitioners rather resistant to mandatory requirements on continuous professional education.

Nonetheless, during the past years, N.M. Tsang and colleagues organized the basic practice teacher course, followed by an advanced module for those who could squeeze the time to participate. The basic course provided the essential knowledge of the 'what, how and why' of practice teaching while the advanced course aimed to develop the practice teachers' ability in becoming a critical reflective practice teacher. The reflective learning approach took the stand that professional knowledge is primarily developed through practice and a systematic analysis of experience. The practitioner, as an action-researcher, constantly tested and critiqued theories of action through situational practice. The team held that the situations faced by the practitioners/practice teachers were uncertain, unique, full of dilemma and value conflict (e.g. traditional culture value clashed with emerging values shaped by the process of modernization). Hence, the practitioner and the service user needed to engage in the process and to construct the problem to be worked on. Classroom learning and the use of co-reflection in small groups were employed.

Knitting research with teaching

To ensure that students develop, sustain and continue to raise their ability to integrate theory and practice, teaching should be underpinned by research activity and findings. A. Yuen Tsang and team built action research into the various projects in the students' practicum. A distinct feature is to involve the service users. New initiatives such as a capacity-building approach among the service users may be introduced. They challenge conventional ways of service delivery, explore new enquiry modes in research; in the process, the concept of the social work educator as an expert has been under scrutiny.

To address the lack of appropriate settings for practice learning in PRC, the department had been successful in securing donations to set up a training centre in Yunnan.

The team is also exploring the development of a culturally sensitive curriculum.

Sustaining quality in the teaching personnel:

Since practice learning pivots on the practicum teacher-student relationship, the facilitation of a culture to nurture the development of such a relationship is deemed important.

To date, APSS has been fortunate that a large proportion of our practicum teachers are University staff. Their work is supported by a team of fieldwork coordinators who facilitate communication and teamwork among students, classroom and practice teachers as well as placement organizations. Staff development courses, such as those mentioned in the discussion of an alternative paradigm above, have been designed to develop the practice teachers continuously. However, with the Government's budget reduction, this model is considered costly and we fear that it will not be sustained.

To prepare for the worse, the department has established a new Practice Learning and Teaching Unit, led by N.M. Tsang, supported by a small team of colleagues from the social work theory and practice team and the fieldwork team. This small group of colleagues is taking on the responsibility of organizng study groups and staff development courses in order to sustain and develop collegial support in teaching. Hopefully, this will continue the enquiry efforts that have begun as well as to support the practice teaching model in whatever form it takes.

PRC has hardly any teaching staff qualified as professional social workers. Hong Kong's attempts to work with our counterparts on this have been discussed in Part 1 above.

Part III: The way forward

Globalization has compressed time and space. People are even more mobile than before. Multi-culture will feature in many of our cities and towns. China will not be an exception, and Hong Kong, a metropolitan city which aims to become a world class financial centre and to serve as the southeastern gateway of China, has indeed an important role to play. Hong Kong, with its goal of developing into a world service centre, will embrace a more multi-cultural population in the future.

Meanwhile Hong Kong and the Mainland societies are rapidly changing and the integration process of the two is accelerating. We anticipate that non-profit making organizations will soon officially move northward to offer services to the people in PRC, and many more social work graduates in Hong Kong will work in the Mainland.

As the world has placed paramount importance on the pursuit of materialistic gain and much less importance on the development of social and spiritual domains, we should lose no time in educating our students in all three domains. Adopting culture-sensitivity training can be a theme that integrates the social, materialistic and spiritual needs of human beings more holistically. However, the cultural theme should be designed so that it must integrate with the curriculum, not as a separate entity with no connection with the rest of the curriculum and the contexts in which we serve. While students should learn and attain cultural competence in working with people from different cultures, they also need to develop as social workers holding on to humanistic values and principles, viewing social work as moral practice.

In addressing themes on values, culture and ethics, we not only need to enable students to contextualize but also to transfer such learning in the understanding and work with service users coming from our own culture as well as other cultures.

In the education of students on values, culture and ethics, we cannot avoid our engagement in the moral domain. My observation is that social work, and social work education, have not been strong in this aspect; thus it is urgent that we research and invest in this area. While we need to continue to understand how western theories impact on eastern practice, we must avoid a narrowly focused, naval gazing approach. We need to adopt an open attitude, research into how theories are generated from the western context, but we also need to learn from other cultures that are apparently less dominant; we need to learn how to help ourselves and our students to critically assimilate knowledge learned to our cultural or multi-cultural context so that we, as well as our students, can work with our service users in a more humanistic, cultural sensitive manner.

Last, but not least, knowledge attained must be shared, exchange, and disseminated at all levels (through projects, joint programmes, research, exchange staff and students), in modes traditional and novel, in printed formats and web-sites, among and across institutions and nations.

To conclude, the above is a preliminary discussion on familism, one major Chinese core culture and its impact on social work practice teaching/learning amidst changing contexts. I have also briefly described responses by a group of academics on issues observed and studied. Last but not least, some suggestions on the way ahead have been outlined.

Notes

1   Advisory Committee on SWT and Manpower Planning: Review of the Roles of Social Work Training Provision on the Training and Development for Social Workers in an Era of Change (Draft) October 2002.

2.   As according to Tsui, M. S's 2004 study, *The Supervisory Relationship of Chinese Social Workers in Hong Kong*, 'qing' refers to the emotional bond build between the supervisor-supervisee. There is an expectation of 'give and take' in the relationship and that the 'exchange/transaction' need not take place immediately.

   'yuan' refers to the belief that being together as supervisor-supervisee is pre-determined by some unexplainable reason, including the arrangement of God; thus they should accept one another's differences.

'*face*' refers to the respect one gives to the other person due to the status this person occupies in one's social network. Giving face is the recognition that the social behaviour is appropriate'. 'Loss of face' arises when the person is unable to live up to the expectation and this would lead to the devaluation of their status in the other's eye. This is often related to 'reciprocity' in the sense that whenever someone gives you 'face', they will expect you to 'give face' in return.

3   The team includes members with qualified social work training.

APPENDIX 1:
Data demonstrating the Magnitude of Social Problems in Hong Kong

- The divorce figures have risen dramatically. The number of Divorce Decrees granted in 2001 was 213. 3% of that of 1991 and 651. 1% of that of 1981. The figure has doubled in the last decade and has increased by over six times in the last two decades.

- Reported battered spouse cases are also on the rise. In 2001, the number of cases was 2,370, which is 97. 5% increase compared to 1,200 reported cases in 1996.

- Between 1995 and 2000, the number of active child abuse cases increased by 95.5%. The number of new cases in 2000 was 123.2% more than the number of recorded cases in 1996 [Child Protection Registry statistical Reports (1996-2001)].

- The growing number of mental health problems is also an issue which warrants serious attention. From 1997 to 1999, there was an annual increase of 13% to 17% in the number of cases of successful suicide in Hong Kong. The situation has been much aggravated by the growing rate of unemployment amidst economic recession.

- Research by the Department of Psychiatry of the Chinese University of Hong Kong showed that over 30% of the 7,000 primary 4 to Form 3 students interviewed had thought of committing suicide during 2001, an increase of 7.9% as compared to a similar research conducted in 1999.

- Juvenile delinquency has been a problem warranting our serious concern for many years. The number of juvenile offenders aged 7 to 15 arrested in 1990-2000 was 6,229, which indicates almost one in a hundred juveniles arrested each year.

- Moreover, the number of Comprehensive Social Security Assistance (CSSA) cases has increased considerably in the last decade. During the period 1991/92 to 2001/02, the increase in all types of cases have been drastic, the table overleaf reflects the situation:

Types of Cases	1991-92	1996-97	2001-02	% increased '91/92 -01/02
Old Age	48020	98765	139288	190. 1
Single Parent Family	4325	13303	29534	582. 9
Ill Health	7966	17948	20082	152. 1
Mentally Ill	4271	7913	9208	115. 6
Unemployment	2248	14964	31602	1305. 8

Note: *The 1991/92 figures were under the Public Assistance Scheme.*
Source: *Census and Statistics Department, Hong Kong* Annual Digest of Statistics, 1998 Edition *(Table 13. 4) and 2002 Edition (Table 14. 4)*

- The number of dependent elderly aged 65 and above also rose considerably from 502,400 or 8. 7% of our population in 1991 to 753,600 or 11. 2% in 2001. It is projected that in 2008 and 2016, the figures will increase to 1. 22m and 1. 62m comprising 16% and 20% of the population respectively. The aging population will undoubtedly result in growing welfare needs and demand for elderly care services.
- The number of one-way permit holders entering Hong Kong also drastically increase by 114% over 10 years (1991 to 2000). While these new entrants to Hong Kong will hopefully become adjusted and assimilated to Hong Kong society, the need for support services such as education at all levels and services during their initial period of settlement cannot be ignored.

8
Service user involvement:
A United Kingdom perspective
on a global opportunity

Graham Ixer

Introduction

This chapter looks at the notion of the service user as someone who is the recipient of social care services and the growing trend towards policies which include service users in the planning, delivery and evaluation of their own services. The focus of all practice learning for professionals in training is to develop sufficient practice knowledge so that the recipients of their endeavour, the service user, get a better deal. Service user involvement can sometimes become confused with public involvement as a much more broader concept instilling a sense of civic duty into one's action. Recent research has highlighted this problem (Newman et al 2004, pp.211-212). Civic duty is more about citizenship than involvement, and a concept little understood in the public sector.

This chapter will consider the critical elements of service user in relation to what a service user is and the nature of their involvement with UK public bodies. The concept of citizenship is reviewed as a major underpinning policy which defines service user in a political context. Little is written about service user as a citizen and an argument will be presented to separate the concept of citizen with service user, not to deny their rights as a citizen, but to actively view service users as something different, therefore requiring specific rather than generalised public and political attention. Its relevant to the theme of this book is critical as all practice learning must now begin to involve service users in such training to ensure its continued relevance to the end product, a 'fit-for-purpose' professional. Waterson and Morris argue that service users must be involved in training to help develop better theoretical understanding, deepen our value base, and develop key skills.

> If done well, students should deepen their understanding and valuing of learning from users about users 'knowledges.' For users the opportunity to contribute and to be heard is, as demonstrated in these two projects, is a way of validating and valuing their experience.(Waterson and Morris, 2005)

Defining social citizenship

Before any sustained attempt to articulate the complexities and issues pertinent to the debate on service user involvement one has to define the notion of 'service user' to contextualise its roots. As mentioned in the introduction, the nature of such involvement is still unclear, despite the prolific public and professional debate on service user involvement (Beresford, 2003; Beresford and Holden, 2000; Morrow, 1999; Robson et al, 2003;), emerging policy from government (BRTF, 2004; DoH, 2002, 2004) and those developing best practice (Turner et al, 2003; SCIE, 2003, 2004a, 2004b; Contact a Family, 2004). However, what is less clear is the nature of what is a service user, who they are and how they are defined. This is the subject of the first part of this paper. To start this debate we need to look at the concept of citizenship.

What is citizenship

In one sense citizenship is something bestowed on us all in the UK – a human right we all enjoy as part of being a member of a nation state or community. However it is not that simple, and the type of citizen we are bestows particular status and responsibility. Some members of society will not be classed as citizens such as some service users, because one such way of defining citizenship is in the balance between individuals exercising their rights and their delivery towards civic duty. Responsibility requires individuals to conform to certain behaviour, production or beliefs and if they fail to do so are relegated to non-citizen status. For example, since 1997 the Labour government's policy on poverty and social exclusion was part driven by the 'New Deal' where 1.25 million people were put back to work (Dwyer, 2004, p.85). New Labour saw work as everyone's' responsibility and made this its main social policy drive on welfare. Levitas (1998) was critical of Labour for too narrowly defining the problem of social exclusion, it was far more complex than ones' inability to work.

Work was seen by the government as the main passport out of poverty and more important, into citizenship: as defined by ones' fulfilling civic duty to its national community. Despite the social strategy for inclusion many service users would never be able to work because of their reliance on welfare due to disability, poverty, poor health, or social dysfunction. This problematised their status as a citizen as they are not fulfilling their duty of production (through work), and therefore, contributing to the state through their taxes. Many service users have felt like third class citizens, never enjoying the same rights and freedoms as others who are able to work and fulfil their state duty. Although some argue that service users make their contribution in other ways, for example, by including them in policy discussion helps develop better social policy and welfare reform (Beresford and Holdon, 2000). Before this debate can be developed further the concept of citizenship needs to be historically contextualised to appreciate the full implications of contemporary theory on service user involvement.

Civic republicanism

The concept of citizenship can be traced back to ancient Greek times where men ruled and citizenship was defined as an exclusive right to all those willing or able to engage or perform in their active duty towards the state. This common commitment towards the state, or more precisely their city was known as 'civic republicanism' and featured individual loyalty to the city as a core characteristic of citizenship. According to the Greek philosopher Aristotle, men can not opt out of their civic duty choose when and how, because they have a moral, legal and political obligation to do what is expected at all times in order to enjoy their status of citizen (Aristotle, 1948). All citizens are 'good citizens' with which one respects and honours and in return are protected and cared for (a right) or called upon to raise arms to defend their nation (a responsibility).

This can be seen in today's society. Who are the good citizens? A good citizen can be classified by those who are selected to become magistrates or are bestowed titles and gifts such as joining the House of Lords or receiving an OBE honour by the Queen. During the Second World War good citizens were those who joined up with the armed forces to give their life for 'God, King and country'. They did not question the morality of their action; it was their duty to their country to give their life. Such duty has changed in today's society and although citizens are unlikely to give up their life for their country so willingly and uncritically, they are nevertheless, subject to the same sense of duty as the cost of being a citizen. They will fulfil their duty to work, obey the law, pay taxes, and participate in the democratic process in voting, in return for receiving health care, education, protection and enjoying being part of society through status bestowed upon them by those who have power to give it.

Liberalism

The concept of liberalism as a model of citizenship developed much later than 4th century republicanism. Heater (1999) discusses how the philosopher Locke in the 17th century proposed an alternative theory of citizenship based on freedom and equality. Such freedom and equality was based on just rights and fair treatment in law, rights to liberty and freedom, and in those days property. Throughout the centuries the expression of rights became more accepted and underpinned the call for arms against oppression and tyranny, in particular, during the seventeenth and eighteenth century revolutions in England, France and North America.

The early forms of liberalism led individuals to think of freedom as a civil right against overbearing state intervention. Individuals were largely responsible for themselves and their status was not based on individual virtue. Therefore it did not matter that an individual did not discharge their responsibilities as others saw it. Individuals would be seen as being different and enjoying in open competition, the right to fair trade, property and other areas for contestation. This was the beginning of capitalism as we know it now. The state plays a limited role for these libertarians. State intervention is limited to ensuring basic civil and political rights (Nozick, 1995). However the criticism of liberalism is that by exercising ones' rights above all others bring the state into chaos, as one person's freedom is another's imprisonment.

One can see this form of liberalism during the 'Margaret Thatcher years.' When Thatcher came to office the Conservatives saw a society too dependent on the state. By allowing freedom and autonomy of will, individuals could compete with each other for the prize of winning the greatest gain. In this sense Thatcher saw freedom linked to economic independence, therefore wealth. A good citizen was one who independently, without state aid, gained economic autonomy. Such 'Thatcher's children' learnt a new virtue and values that propagated the principle of individual autonomy – 'I work for my own wealth and have no responsibility to others, irrespective of how my action affects others'. Consequently the freedom gained by Thatcher's children led to oppression of others and state dependency from the majority of those who were affected by such outcomes. The poor became poorer, public services became more limited as services were constricted to ability to pay. A new virtue entered our vocabulary – 'We all have the ability and opportunity to make it, only if we really want to we will'. Such sentiment was the lasting legacy of Thatcher that new Labour began a journey of dismantling.

Social citizenship

According to Marshall (1992) there is no universal principle defining citizenship in what it requires or gives. His theory of citizenship has three key elements that appear as relevant today and relevant to the time when he first wrote about it in the 1940s. There are three key elements to citizenship: civil, political and social. Citizenship is something that is given to certain members of a national community. All those that possess such status are equal with respect to the rights and duties with which such status is bestowed. What these rights and duties give is unclear and often changing which is why some citizens often find themselves treated unequally, such as service users, even though they still believe themselves as equal citizens.

The first element of citizenship is civil right and means ones right to individual liberty. This is enshrined in our human rights legislation, the right to freedom of speech and faith, the right to own property and the right to justice. The right to be treated fairly by the law. The second is political right. This means the right to be part of the democratic process, the right to vote, be elected and the right to have power in directing a community on behalf of others. The third is social right. This is a much more wide ranging right as it means the right to be included in society in what ever that means. Being included could mean the same right to security and protection, economic welfare and social heritage as mainstream society enjoy. It is the right to civilised society and enjoying the same standards of life given to the majority.

Many service users are excluded from exercising their full social rights and therefore under Marshall's notion of citizenship are not equal. Such inequality can also be seen in other groups of people made vulnerable by their circumstance such as asylum seekers, refugees, travelling people, people incarcerated in prison, homeless people, people infected by HIV and Aids and people from black and ethnic minority communities. It is because citizenship is so unclearly defined that leads to those recognised as citizens deciding who has equal status. The consequence of such inequality is an abuse of power and prejudice. This can be seen in those who are given low status or whose citizenship is subject to immigration restrictions, such as asylum seekers. Such people find it difficult to integrate in mainstream society. Despite the shortage of doctors in the UK there are 1000 unemployed refugee doctors unable to secure work because they cannot achieve the language proficiency test required to enter the General Medical Council's register. Many are held in detention (Clarke, 1994).

Citizenship and the wider agenda

Citizenship is a complex subject too broad for this paper. However, citizenship touches us all as a process of belonging and social inclusion as a process of exclusion and oppression. Our social status determines what side of the fence we may reside and therefore rights we enjoy or lose. Cockburn (2005) uses the example of children's participation to argue the dilemma caused by exclusion from authorities who see some children as competent and others as not. In representative democracy civic engagement for children can mean being excluded because the focus of policy development is on the construction of the policy and not the engagement of those who are recipients of social policy. Cockburn argues that unless we refocus our policy agenda on 'engagement, co-construction and partnership' (p.215) we in danger of paying 'lip service' to the civic involvement agenda. Citizen participation is a key element of all local based regeneration policy (Alcock, 2004)

There are social barriers to full citizenship often obscured by paternal policies promoting individual dependency of the state rather than individual freedom from the state and empowerment to determine ones' own life. Alcock (1997) looks at how poverty is measured as a way of excluding some and including others all of which help to define citizenship – those that are included and those that are not.

Citizenship is also a gendered concept (Lister, 2002). Men have dominated the critiques of citizenship and how it should be defined. We have a patriarchal welfare state where women are second-class citizens (Pateman, 1989). Women are not equal citizens in that they do not enjoy the same civil, political and social rights as men. Equal protection from domestic violence or fair treatment in court in a rape trial are two such examples.

Disability is also another barrier to citizenship. Barnes et all (2002, 2003) provide sufficient critiques on disability to suggest that disabled people are seen as a problem to society, their condition or impairment is medicalised. Although the social model of disability has helped to empower disabled people to challenge discrimination, and despite legislative changes, their rights are still being withdrawn. Those people on 'direct payments' have to fight for equal rights to employment, education and services compared to their non-disabled colleagues. Society is still discriminatory towards disabled people, partly because society only views life though the prism of the able-bodied person. Such attitudes and values serve to continue the isolation and exclusion many disabled people experience.

Race and ethnicity are other forms of social exclusion from full citizenship. Brubaker (1992) argues that many black and ethnic minority citizens are disadvantaged. They cannot enjoy the same rights to welfare as their white counterparts, which may be due to racism and not being seen as part of an idealised and racialised national norm. They are different therefore not part of their community. However, if this is to be tackled effectively one needs to go beyond the 'black and white' divide, this is too simplistic. A more complex understanding of race is needed that includes religious and cultural practices. Black communities are not homogenous groups but often brought together through their culture affinity for each other from a shared experience of racism. The government's debate on asylum policy is one of the largest single policy issues that fuel the divide on those who can belong as citizens and those that cannot.

Globalised citizenship

Finally there is the notion of national citizenship and globalised citizenship (Tambini, 2001). The UK is part of Europe and as such enjoys certain rights, such as equal human rights, fair trade etcetera. Workers and communities no longer have to remain static in one nation state but have free movement across states. Economic migration has led to changes in demography. Where for example, there is a shortage of social workers in the UK and excess in Spain, it is purely a matter of redistribution of the workforce. However, this brings us into conflict with cultural barriers of belonging and sameness. For example, in those professions that are regulated such as doctors find that many overseas doctors wishing to work in the UK are thwarted because they fail the language test and leads to them returning to their home state (LfPN, 2003).

Globalisation has brought about vast changes in economies and fiscal policies. The speed in which world trade has overcome traditional markets and large transnational corporations (TNC) move from one labour market to another to maximise profit are examples of such change. This has resulted in industry decline in some countries such as manufacturing in the UK and increases in other countries where labour is cheaper such as Asian countries.

This invisible freedom to move from one country to another with financial ease is not paralleled in the labour market. Labour is traditionally fixed through immigration control, culture and language barriers. Movement of labour can neither compete nor follow the trend and direction of industry change in closing existing markets and opening new ones. It is the TNC that can move quickly and globally. The consequence is an unstable labour force and more importantly, exclusion to the full benefits of globalisation in the profit and success of TNCs.

Many of these issues serve to heighten the plight for service users because without dismantling global and national barriers, understanding their significance and challenging their disadvantage will lead to paying lip service to service user involvement. This is because social barriers are dimensions of human agency that we have to consider when thinking about who is a service user. A service user is all of those dimensions and in many ways experience multiple forms of disadvantage because they are excluded as a service users and often oppressed because they are black, a woman, disabled or a foreign national. Service users must be seen more holistically, this means including all the dimensions to their human experience. A service user is first a person second, their need is not the problem rather than the system, and third, they are equal citizens because their contribution to society although different is equal.

In this sense citizenship is about power and in order for a service user to gain equal citizen status they need equal power to determine for themselves their own way of life and it not being conditional on meeting certain state obligations such as employment. For example, they cannot work and earn money, which would give them independence without it affecting their social benefit entitlements. In this sense they can never be equal citizens. Service users are also members of the public and as such, health have developed new structures and frameworks to enable the public to get involved in the development, delivery and monitoring of health services. Although service users are members of the public, in relation to involvement they should be seen differently to the public, as the public are part of the problem of disadvantaging service users. It is the public who maintain the barriers furthering the continuance of discrimination experienced by service users. Consequently we cannot treat service users the same as the public, they need to be treated differently if we are to have any success in bringing down public centred and maintained barriers to achieve full inclusion.

However, even in examining globalised citizenship we are constrained in the literature by a Eurocentric view as argued by Taylor (1996). Citizenship is debated and understood from a Eurocentric perspective denying a more international context involving race and ethnicity.

The nature of the term service user involvement

Having explored the issues related to the term service user the following will look at the activity service users are recruited to engage. Firstly, it should be pointed out that service users do not like the term 'service user' or in fact other terms such as client, customer, student, resident, and others that label them distinctly apart from public and citizen. Such is the disempowering affect this has, many champions of 'user involvement' acknowledge these terms as barriers (Beresford, 1994). Also service users are not a homogenous group, they are as diverse as the public. In this chapter the term service user is a recognised term to mean those people using social care services despite the language widely rejected by service users.

What is involvement

This is a difficult concept to define as it means different things to different people. However, some organisations such as the Social Care Institute for Excellence (SCIE) have tried to adopt the concept of involvement in a more active partnership with service users. As such they use the term service user participation. This is something that British government is also beginning to adopt (BRTF, 2004). Participation infers a more active and empowering role for the service user whereas 'involvement' limits itself to mere attendance to an event or activity. In other words you are there with little meaningful activity or purpose (Newman et al, 2004, p.203).

The concept of participation has led to wider debate. Boyden and

Ennew (1997) separate two distinctions between participation in the sense of 'taking-part' or 'being-present', e.g. latent participation and participation in the sense of 'knowing that one's actions are taken note of and may be acted upon. This is referred to 'active participation'. Other terms such as service user engagement are also used to imply more active participation. Although could be argued - 'What's in a name'? It is absolutely critical that language is understood. These concepts are still developing and lead to a growing debate on service user involvement as an activity where the service user has equal power to engage in the activity and influence the process. However, real power is unlikely to be achieved on the part of the service user without having control over their own decisions – this means having their own budget.

Accessing service users

UK public sector engagement with service users has been a dominant feature of the way health and social care services are currently planned, delivered and monitored. As part of the government's drive for local accountability, service users are invited to be involved and planners and service deliverers are expected to involve them. Therefore planners are always inviting service users to sit on committees, groups and fora, or to take part in consultations as part of giving and hearing the service user voice on matters that concern them. However, because such work is not strategically coordinated across the UK, many service uses either do not get involved or the same people are always involved, or such people are over consulted. Many organisations do manage to overcome these difficulties and achieve successful genuine service user involvement because they have service users involved at the start, planning the consultation or leading it. Organisations such as 'Shaping our Lives National User Network' (SOLNUN) have made an enormous contribution to user involvement because they are led by service users. One of their main assets is to advise other organisations accessing and involving service users. Consequently, consultations run by SOLNUN are more likely to seek the voice of service users as service users themselves control access.

The issue for planners is not so much how to access service

users but more what type of service user is required? Given service users are not a homogenous group how do we reach the group we want? In addition to the discussion on citizenship in the first part of this chapter, service users can be categorised by the way they receive services and seen as the disabled group, the mental health group, etcetera.

There are those service users that are easy to access and engage, and who currently use services. These might be disabled people, children or people on direct payment who are able to articulate their experience and expertise of being a service user. They might also be people who have used care services in the past. Then there are those users of services who are hard to engage because of communication needs. These might be very young people, people with learning difficulties or older people with dementia and severely disabled people with sensory impairments. They all share experience of using services but their ability to articulate it clearly will be different. The next category would be service users that are 'seldom heard' or 'hard to reach' because of being excluded from mainstream society. These are be people who do not want to get involved because they are subject to state intervention and have had their children taken away, service users who are in prison and subject to restriction of liberty or black service users who are marginalized as part of experiencing discrimination. Lastly those service users who currently do not use services but need them. These might be those people placed on the margins of society such as travelling people, refugees and asylum seekers, homeless, those disaffected such as runaway teenagers or those who do not meet the eligibility criteria for services but nonetheless, have a need.

All these groups can broadly be seen as service users but will be viewed differently by society and therefore receive the benefits of society differently. Organisations and governments do not acknowledge the potential range of service user available and therefore miss an opportunity to gain greater breadth in service user involvement. The challenges confronting any organisation wanting to engage people in the hard to reach or engage groups will experience enormous challenges but it is only if there is a genuine commitment and belief in diversity in service user involvement will organisations find ways to overcome these barriers. Evidence thus far suggests that organisations are either unwilling or unable to engage these groups (SCIE, 2004).

Collective representation verses individual voice

Who does the service user represent? When service users are asked to sit on a committee or become involved in an event are they representing themselves, a particular group of service users or the entire service user sector? It is difficult to answer these questions as there is no one answer. Where a service user is representing an organisation it is straight forward as they are in a representational role.

Representing a particular constituency is more problematic. It is the contention in the following diagram in Fig.1 that there are three layers of representation. The first is the micro-layer where the individuals represent themselves, and the context is personal. An individual represents themselves and has one voice. The second is the macro-layer where they represent the concept of service user as a global stakeholder of using services. This may be a particular type of service user, group or organisation and have many voices. In this their representation is not based on doing what is right for all service users, as that would be impossible, but adhering to certain principles and values. This could be the values of a rights based approach for all service users. These two layers are joined together by a political layer that moves between them both depending on the context and need. The political layer is a social construction of reality given to service users by those in power who chose to engage them. Service users are engaged through a political imperative as part of a much larger agenda on civic involvement. It was Tony Blair who said, 'we need to recreate the bonds of civic society and community' (Blair 1997) that led to a sea change in pubic involvement and now service user involvement. Its entire activity is driven by political ideology and not as service users might believe, core professional values of involvement. The political imperative is needed to achieve an end that might not always be in the best interest of the service user but nevertheless, needs to be understood if professional engagement with service user involvement is to be successful.

Much of new legislation in England pose a duty on the public sector to involve the public in the planning, delivery and monitoring of public services. A good example of this is that through the Health Act 2002 a new body called the Commission for Patient and Public Involvement was set up and charged with the responsibility of creating 560 public and patient involvement forums. Members of the public are recruited to these groups who have a direct inspectorial and monitoring role over the quality of all health services (primary and secondary care).

Fig. 1

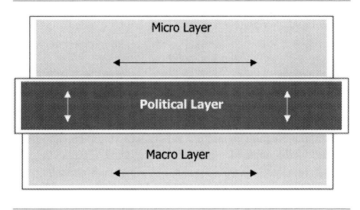

Valuing involvement

One of the biggest contentions for service users is whether or not they are going to be paid for their involvement. It is a contradiction in itself because if we follow the political citizenship line then individuals become involved out of civic duty. This is their contribution to society, democracy and freedom. However, service user groups argue that their involvement is different to civic involvement because their involvement is a contribution of expertise. Consequently expertise should be paid for. This creates another barrier, as many service users are low paid, unemployed or living on social benefits. If they receive payment it could affect their social benefits and would certainly be taxable. Also many service users are not given expenses in full. A disabled person who employs an assistant would have to have their full costs of travel and assistant paid as well. Such high cost often precludes some employers extending an invitation to them.

Payment is clearly a way of valuing involvement but to many service users its more, it is a right. Valuing involvement can come in many ways and does not have to always be seen in terms of economic gain. The Social Care Institute for Excellence has undertaken much research in this area and their findings point to other factors that need to be considered (SCIE 2004a).

Organisations engaging service user involvement do so without too much thought and planning about exactly what it is they want. Further, there is little evidence to suggest that the voice of service users is being heard. More important the question for the service user of 'What's in it for me?' is never contemplated. Service users want to know that they are making a useful contribution, they are being heard and genuinely valued. Many service users choose not to get involved again because of the lip service paid to involvement. To overcome this many organisations are developing their strategy on service user involvement. An informal network of regulators across health and social care have been meeting to develop core principles of involvement (Participation Steering Group 2004) and recently these principles have bee recommended in a high level report to government by the Better Regulation Taskforce who wrote a report on service user participation in adult care (BRTF 2004). Society is unlikely to believe in service user involvement until it is understood better and is valued as an equal contribution to that of non-service user involvement.

Analysis

There are many examples around the world where service user involvement does not need any particular or different thinking or planning as it is part of the main infrastructure for delivering community health and social care services in countries such as Angola, Chile and Brazil (Meads 2004). Public involvement is an excepted norm and part of delivering essential public services. Because in the UK professionals have historically controlled how services should be delivered they have acted as the gatekeepers to those who are allowed into the professions. Barriers are maintained through education and professional registration requirements. Those institutions responsible for regulating the professions have been reluctant to relinquish power under the defence of 'public protection'. It therefore becomes increasingly difficult for a service user to sit alongside a professional and share their expertise on equal terms.

The UK has traditionally valued professional expertise more than service user expertise. Firstly, because it is only recently and through organisations such as Social Care Institute for Excellence that service user experience is framed in a context of expertise and secondly, professionals view expertise hierarchically. Power is given to a level of hierarchy through the seniority of post and the length of training. An example of this is in the UK high court system. In giving evidence to a high Court judge a social worker whose evidence is based on many years of contact with a particular service user will still not be considered an expert witness, compared with a child psychiatrist who has trained over a longer period of time then a social worker. This is nothing to do with understanding the child better but merely the length of their training. Such a position is unsustainable in modern society but still part of the cultural fabric of the English judiciary.

This example supports the assertion that despite all best efforts, genuine service user involvement is hard to achieve. This is because mainstream society does not want it otherwise those barriers marginalising service users would be brought down by those in power to do so. Service users although are the public, in many cases are not part of civic society for all the reasons presented earlier therefore, must be treated differently to the public. The public are part of the problem of service user exclusion. Positive efforts need to be made to bring down the barriers and build an organisational culture that genuinely puts service user at the heart if this is what society genuinely wants. To achieve this the first and most fundamental act on the part of any organisation seeking service user involvement needs to clearly analyse why they want service user involvement and what benefits it brings. They need to be honest with themselves.

An organisation needs to be honest and confident in asserting why and where it needs service user involvement. It may wish for limited involvement for certain parts of its activities such as consultations on policy, or it may wish for service user involvement in its governance. For service user involvement to be successful an organisation needs to articulate its involvement in a transparent way that staff know and understand, but more important, service users understand why they are becoming involved, how, where and what's in it for them. Not only will this make for successful involvement in relation to good outcomes and ethical practice, but also it brings civic involvement and service user involvement together for the first time.

Conclusion

Service users need to be treated differently to the public, because the public are part of the problem in excluding and discriminating against service users. By treating service users differently, by being proactive in empowering the relationship between all participants, the service user is able to become involved more on equal terms. By participating on equal terms ensures the planning and delivery of care services are better tailored to meet the needs of the service user. |This produces better outcomes for the service user. Practice learning students need to understand this process so they can contribute to sharing power with service users in a way that delivers better outcomes for the service user and the care provider.

Notes

1. Direct payments are an alternative to state control care. People are given their own individualised funding to directly control purchasing their own social care

2. An example of this from England is the Government's setting up of a new statutory body, the Commission for Public and Patient Involvement, whose task was to recruit members of the public to sit on forums for each Health Trust. They were given powers of inspection through the Health Act.

9

Inquiring: Invasion or invitation? Questioning the questioning process

Elaine Hume

Therapist's' questions must be disciplined to serve purpose in circumstance. If the purpose is not therapeutic, the question is better not asked. If the effect is not therapeutic, the question better not be asked the next time. (Dillon, 1990, p.45)

Introduction

Australian society is unique, challenging and dynamic yet shares many of its qualities with other societies around the world. It has the extremes of a long indigenous history and recent history of multiple layers of migration and cultural diversity. It is a country with no land neighbours, yet large enough for its countrymen to live thousands of miles apart and feel isolated. Economic resources are not evenly distributed while educational and occupational opportunities vary. Social work is one sub-culture within this wider mix. To be consistent in self-appraisal it must overcome cross-cultural issues in communicating social work values, standards and expectations to new 'immigrants' (not only geographical but academic and professional) and be sensitive to the new cultures we are encountering. Methods tried and tested in this context are transferable to any other mix of cultures and traditions, and to the global stage.

This chapter focuses on the small environment of the interview and the questioning processes we use, yet proposes that the tool developed has relevance to the widest of teaching contexts, social work around the globe.

Broad issues of communication

There is a dynamic in conversation or communication where, with numerous devices such as body language, emphasis, metaphor and silence, the message is exchanged. Participants advance and retreat, give each other the floor, take turns, ask, answer, (and even say just as much by not speaking at all). There are already significant barriers to communication and these are exacerbated within the hierarchy of the interview, whether practitioner and client or the supervisor/supervisee relationship. Gender, age, cultural diversity and various religious and socio-economic factors will influence a student or practitioner's willingness and availability to accommodate criticism and guidance.

The process of inquiry

My thesis is that responsibility for the outcome of any inquiry lies not in the detail of the answers but in the choice of the question style. In order to gauge the therapeutic strengths of a question one needs to be able to measure the invasive or invitational qualities of any inquiry. Dillon's words above apply to therapeutic contexts, but equally to any inquiry, be it counselling, supervisory or managerial. These other contexts though not therapeutic all demand a high level of insight into one's intentions, an awareness of the impact of what one says and an expectation of the outcome of any inquiry. Linguistics can help student, supervisor and manager to learn, and to monitor their communication and inquiry skills.

Dealing with the novice

The broadest of professional principles and values such as self-determination, freedom, justice and equity do not give the student something to hold onto in the early learning stages. A student will often focus on the information to be gathered in an interview rather than the relationship to be developed. The intent behind the content of an answer will be ignored in favour of a fact or anticipated response. The social work values and techniques proposed by the supervisor or training institution must be tangible and based on a valid argument, rather than imposed from a position of power. Introducing the profession to an unknown or different culture will be more successful where it is based on a set of labels or criteria, that is applicable to the speech background of both participants and not biased by the supervisor's own dominant culture. This argues for new criteria for judging the professional practice of the student or new practitioner. Such scrutiny can be useful beyond student/supervisor discussions and applies across all areas where the question of communication and sensitivity to another perspective exists. Mature practitioners and supervisors can re-gauge their own questioning skills within inquiry, supervisory and managerial settings.

What Linguistics has to offer

Linguistics provides universal criteria, applicable to all languages that can focus on the sensitivity and efficacy of the inquiry process. It provides a common language to consider how to develop preferred or 'necessary' styles of inquiry and fosters in individuals common criteria to apply to their own unique style and skills. The most significant aspect of this common language is that it demonstrates respect for the 'other' perspective. Such resources are extremely useful in assisting the student or practitioner to bring to life the dynamics of an inquiry and learn to appreciate 'The How' of professional practice.

Hume Inquiry Tool

The 'Hume Inquiry Tool' relies on Linguistics to label the questioning process. It is a chart or tool that focuses on the questions asked and the extent to which the inquirer advances into, and withdraws from, the space of the interviewee. The tool provides substance and reference to the questions around 'Did I ask that question the way I wanted? Did I get the outcome I wanted?, Will/would I ask it that way again? Was it heard the way I intended or did I trigger an unexpected response?' It asks if this is what the practitioner wanted and leaves scope to find a preferred alternative way of questioning. It links three issues, placing the attention on what was asked and linking it to the Values, Ethics and Culture behind the choosing. It relates impact to outcome, intention to results, and accommodates investigative processes with the issues of relationship. Providing the background to this chart and an explanation of its creation belies the simplicity of its use. It requires little recording, is readily internalized by the newest of students and practitioners, and becomes a ready platform of review.

The tool brings together the work of three areas of linguistics studies:

1. Labov and Fanshell (1979) provide a dynamic concept of the inquiry, supervisory session or cross-cultural engagement. They argue that in any human interaction each participant enters the relationship with their own areas of knowledge and perspective. (These can be termed pres-suppositionary pools- 'what I already know and am expecting to happen'). It is the interchange of views and information that produces a common area; these concepts are A, B and D events:

    A-events, known only to the Speaker,
    B-events, known only to the Hearer,
    D-events, disputable (known/seen) by both.

    As an interaction proceeds there is growth in the D events, (even if it is of knowledge that other knowledge isn't being shared), the exchange may be equal or one sided. Participants might not be equally capable, willing, and generous in their contribution. It reminds us the interchange is moving through time.

2. Cederborg et al (2000) studied the questioning of children in alleged sexual abuse investigations. They demonstrated that choice of inquiry style influenced the information provided, the manner of its presentation and showed the influence the Inquirer brought to bear on the interviewee. Courts of law considered information was tainted, and no longer the interviewee's story. Evidence was contaminated by the suggestive nature of leading and loaded questions. The four categories of question recognised were:

    *   *Suggestive utterances.* These are stated in such a way that the

inquirer strongly communicates what response is expected (eg: 'He forced you to do that, didn't he?') or they assume details that have not been revealed by the child (eg: Child: 'We laid on the sofa. ' Inquirer: 'He laid on you or you laid on him?')

- *Option-posing utterances.* These focus the child's attention on details or aspects of the alleged incident that the child has not previously mentioned, asking the child to affirm, negate, or select an investigator-given option using recognition memory processes, but do not imply that a particular response is expected.

- *Directive utterances.* These refocus the child's attention on details or aspects of the alleged incident that the child has already mentioned, providing a category for requesting additional information using 'When/ where did that happen' questions (cued recall).

- *Invitations.* Utterances, including questions, statements, or imperatives, prompting free-recall responses from the child. Such utterances do not delimit the child's focus except in a general way (for example, 'Tell me everything that happened'), or use details disclosed by the child as cues (eg, 'You mentioned that he touched you. Tell me everything about the touching').

This affirms the previous study by Sternberg et al (1997), which demonstrated that open ended questioning, used as entry into the inquiring context:

- Enabled the Interviewee to part with a far greater amount of information, and
- That information was far less influenced by the inquirer's phrasing.

(For example more information given with far less contamination))

3. Dillon (1990, pp.177-207) provides a sequence of non-question techniques that call forth information or action. These form an extension and counterbalance to the Cederborg et al. work. I will adapt these categories and use the following ones:
   - *Silent pauses* – saying nothing
   - *Fillers, phatics and passe* – (indicating attentive interest, or encouraging additional speech, briefly exclaiming a reaction

– 'aha', 'mmmm'… that invite the story to be continued)
- Statements are of 4 kinds:
    o *Declarative* – 'That doesn't help much'
    o *Reflective* – 'No-one understood how sad you were'
    o *Of mind* – 'I think you were hard done by'
    o *Of interest* – 'I'd be interested to hear how you go'.
- *Practitioner reddition* is information giving – personal, procedural, professional or theoretical on the part of the counsellor/Interviewer.
- *Speaker questions* are the inquirer's responses to the speaker/client's questions.

The tool in use

A hierarchy of inquiry techniques is presented. Those at the top invade the space of the client; suggesting, leading and thereby imposing assumptions and expectations of the answers to be provided. In the middle, pauses, fillers and phatics acknowledge and commend the client for participating without placing barriers to the telling of the story. (Yet it can be a student's perspective that he or she was ineffectual or not directive enough because they 'just' let the client talk.) Towards the lower end, the inquirer parts with opinion or information, sharing with the client, not just asking for more. Practice tells me that in this very process of giving (or at least not demanding more), the inquirer is often given more than could be demanded. Information provided by the inquirer can empower the client; as it demonstrates a sharing in the process, models putting oneself at risk even, and shows respect and appreciation by repaying in kind.

These categories can be charted through the progress of an inquiry. The *Inquirer's* sequences of utterances are marked. The manner in which the questioner probes or shares can be tracked, and can record the movement of the inquiry through time and each actor's space. This is a chart that will let us plot the flow of inquiry.

The appendix provides samples of the chart with the overlapping vortex of Labov and Fanshell given diagrammatic form. The overlying crossing lines call up each actor's pre-suppositionary pools that will drive forward or impede the growth in common ground as the inquiry proceeds (or doesn't). Secondly the tool is shown in its usable form, ready to be copied, ready for use. There then follows some examples of interviewing styles and their charted forms. These clearly demonstrate the different patterns of inquiry. The sample of a naïve or student's inquiry reflects a less fluid and intuitive pattern than with the experienced Inquirer. The student's focus on asking for the next fact inhibits being available to hear and respond to the previous answer, and cuts across the potential of a developing relationship.

Such a chart of the inquirer's movement can be used to:

- Demonstrate visually what is often a cognitive and emotional interaction.
- Demonstrate the way the inquirer enters the space of the client, or invites the client to advance into common territory or even into the counsellor's space.
- Link certain questioning styles to certain parts of the inquiry.
- Account for a counsellor's sense of control/discomfort by reviewing the types of movement in the inquiry.
- Reflect the skills (or their absence) of the Inquirer.
- Weave the pattern of each specific counselling context to demonstrate the pattern of a certain counsellor.
- Link the changes in style and stages of the relationship of Inquirer and client, especially over a series of interviews.
- Provide comparison between counsellors where there is reason to standardize styles of inquiry.
- Demonstrate visually whether there are common patterns for specific topics or issues irrespective of the individual therapist

Opportunities

This tool will not prescribe what the style should be, but pattern it … and thereby demonstrate the pattern that emerges for a certain worker, a certain context, inquiry goal or theoretical construct. After a few occasions of reviewing an interview using the chart, pen and paper, it easily translates into a review that occurs as you walk from the interview, gauging the movement of information and the relationship that has occurred. The discussion can then flow on to linking this process to the theoretical values and cultural prescriptions that lie beneath. This leaves you free to ask and answer the questions such as 'Is this what best reflects my values', 'Am I comfortable being heard this way', 'Is it appropriate to my theoretical construct?' 'Where do the gaps appear between theory and practice?' 'Should I be more invasive to carry out a mandated role?'

There will be contexts where:

- Intrusive questions are meant to be asked, (mandatory inquiries, statutory benefit applications, the challenging supervisory session).
  There is a need to standardize styles of inquiry – research, mandatory procedures such as child abuse or court related practice.
- The theoretician might determine never to ask a question, (certain psychotherapies).
- The counsellor is intending to model the risks of sharing information, or where the social worker is developing a narrative with the client in a collaborative manner.

Linguistics, in fact, is demonstrating to many SocialWork practitioners what they already know, and providing them with the language to label what has been known intuitively. It provides the opportunity to give substance to intuition and order to good practice. Here is a tool that questions the questioner. It forms a very close link between the manner of asking questions, the 'goal' of the inquiry and the relationship that develops within that inquiry.

In summary

While this tool was originally developed to assist the student social worker to reflect on the minutiae of the asking process, the same benefits are available to the supervisor. Where social work must attend to cross-cultural issues this tool provides a common ground based on respect for the other perspective. 'Are you aware how invasive that question was?', or conversely 'that that style of question brings no authority with it?' These can be charted, depersonalized in the process of using the chart. Authority lies in the inquirer's respect for the domain of the other, not in imposing from a position of power a certain set of rules. It enables the interviewer to demonstrate respect for the client's domain. It enables the supervisor, whether of students, practitioners, peers or self, to ask what was intended, was it achieved, and at what cost to the relationship of the actors involved. In this way, this tool can translate from the small world of any individual Australian interview to the broadest applications of teaching and counselling around the globe.

APPENDIX

Chart and overlay

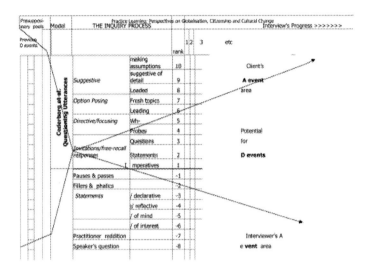

Chart

				10																			

Sample interviews

First, a naïve interview that shows an inexorably invasive process. One can imagine that there are circumstances where such probing would be intended, but not commonly in the therapeutic context. The second demonstrates an Inquirer who is more aware of the process, able to wait for the information to be provided and so gives the client space to talk.

Sample 1

(naïve or student)
1. Hello I'm. .
2. Who told you to talk to me?
3. What is it about?
4. When did that happen?
5. What caused it?
6. Were you all drinking alcohol at the time?
7. Shouldn't you all have known better?
8. Wasn't there something you could do to avoid it?
9. Who is going to look after him now?
10. Will you stop work to look after him?

Sample 2

My name is Sue.
I've been told you wanted to speak to me.
Aha aha.
It can be difficult in these surroundings.
No.
It won't be discussed with anyone from your work.
Yep. Yep.
Was that the first time?...Yep. Yep....

'Student' sample chart

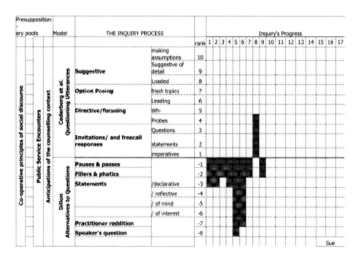

'Experienced' sample chart

10
Globalized consumer culture: Its implications for social justice and practice teaching in social work
Fred H. Besthorn

We get better and better at making new and complicated things in organized ways we call economies. We figure out who is powerful and who is less so. We have come to a time when making things at a desperate pace seems essential to our worth—indeed a time when we have become things ourselves. We are worth for what we can sell ourselves. Like some Frankenstein system, our creation redefines and consumes us. The deeper tragedy is that this monster redefines and consumes the Earth as well. (**Thomas Keefe**)

Introduction

At this point in history humanity has enough material resources to meet the basic needs of every person on earth. We have the capacity to enhance health care, sanitation, and meet concerns for cleaner environments in most areas. Nevertheless, a cursory look around during this period of rising international crises, growing alarms of global warming, and severe shortages of clean water, shows just how far we are from realizing these goals. The world community is instead becoming a global village of two distinct and separated groups of people. There is the first world of wealth, opulence, and conspicuous consumption and a third world of deprivation, poverty, and subsistence living.

The stratification of the world community is no longer constrained within national borders. It is no longer just an issue of rich northern economies versus struggling nations in the global south. Increasingly, one can find relatively insulated pockets of wealth surrounded by ever deepening chasms of misery in most countries around the world. Many of the world's nations are now being forced to adopt a kind of winner-take-all globalized financial system where the goal is to get as much as one can according to his or her own greed quotient. Selfishness, self-indulgence, and rampant materialism have become cardinal values for many of the world's citizens. The relentless psychological marathon of yearning and having increasingly drives the world social system. But, its darker underbelly keeps us perpetually unhappy, chronically sick in body and soul, obese, and neurotically yearning for the *spirit of the buy*. Our lives are lived in anticipation of the next purchase which is always just out of reach but always immanently possible. But we are, by most accounts, as poor in collective, meaningful connection as the Afghanis and Iraqis are in money. We literally are buying our way into deep peril, poverty and emotional destruction while believing *this is what we ought to be doing*. We in the developed world are also endeavoring to taint the world with our peculiar malady. While we are spending ourselves into extinction we are also enslaving the vast percentage of the world's workforce and expropriating the lion's share of their country's natural resources to insure our demise.

Today everything is for sale—politics, sex, love, marriage, and gizmos and promises of every size and description. We seem never quite content, ever on the search—spiritual searches, romantic searches, experiential searches, searches for meaning, searching for the better deal. We have become the quintessence of the consumer culture that enfolds us.

Buy and Be Happy?

Most of us have been seduced by the delusion of the new world order—that having more wealth and possessions are essential to happiness. And yet, data increasingly suggests that more wealth and consumer goods, beyond a certain level, do not lead to happy or satisfied lives. This presentation will look at the problem of the globalized consumptive ethos and its implications for human well-being. It shall also address how the profession's commitment to social justice is influenced by the consumptive emphasis of traditional social justice paradigms and will offer an alternative approach to social justice and its implication for social work practice teaching. It will suggest strategies regarding how social work practice teaching might address the materialistic values and practices of late modern, consumeristic capitalism and how a change in that perspective might truly improve the quality of life of communities and the planet.

The consumer driven economy of the western world generally, and of the United States particularly, is based on a multi-faced constellation of values and ideologies about ourselves and the world we inhabit. In the main, these values minimize the relevance of intuitive, interpretive, communal, and quality of life aspects of experience in preference for the economic enterprise of consumption and amassing material wealth. The cost of industrialized consumption is externalized and not considered in the price of consumer products. Consumer culture assumes nations and economies must grow incessantly or perish. The truly happy and fulfilled person is one who accrues as much material wealth and pleasure as possible.

To have, to have not, longing and desire, abundance and scarcity, stuff and no-stuff—these are the real and un-realized essences of consumerism in America and increasingly in the rest of the world. Global capitalism has become simply the economic tool that breathes life into that moment of sheer delight when we acquire something we've not had. The giddy anticipation that holds us spellbound before the glittering incantations of *a better and brighter tomorrow*—a future resplendent with more stuff. Most of the world's work force is employed in the business of producing commodities and services. To paraphrase Rossenblatt (1999), consumer products travel, bringing both themselves and their desire to have more to countries that have less - and those who have nothing - so that one glorious day, even these places of desolation can, through spending and getting, experience the insane, but intoxicating enigma of having while always feeling they have not.

Modern culture is bombarded with messages to spend, spend, spend and in the process one shall find real worth, deep satisfaction, and a genuinely meaningful life (Kasser, 2002). Multicolor ads flash across TV and computer screens and invade our lives in every imaginable way. Latter day huskers implore us to buy everything from sexual enhancing performance supplements to personalized names for recently discovered stars. We are even told that the best defense against encroaching terrorism is to go to the mall and spend our money. Although the content may be different the message is the same: happiness and security are found in the purchasing of things, the ownership of 'stuff', and the status such things supposedly bring to us.

While no one would argue that some basic level of material comfort is necessary for essential human needs; it is quite another thing to say that higher levels of material accumulation lead to ever increasing levels of satisfaction and happiness. To the contrary, recent research (Besthorn, 2002; Brown, 2001; Cohen, 2003; Crocker & Linden, 1998; Frank, 1999; Goodwin, Ackerman & Kiron, 1997; Kasser, 2002, Myers, 2000; Rossenblatt, 1999; Wentz, 2001; Westra & Werhane, 1998) is suggesting overwhelmingly that materialistic values actually detract from well-being and quality of life experiences, such as self-expression, intimate relationships, and sense of community.

The death of personal well-being.

In recent years, investigators working in various fields have begun to assess the cost of a materialistic lifestyle. What they have found is startling. The reality is that people in the western world and increasingly in the developing world (Diener & Oishi, 2000; Khanna & Kasser, 2001; Saunder & Munro, 2000) are generally not adapting well to consumerist culture and are exhibiting rather destructive ways of living. In short, materialism is associated with relatively low levels of well-being and psychological health, as well as relatively high levels of narcissism, depression, and anxiety. Indeed, evidence suggests that aspiring to greater wealth and material possessions is associated with increased personal unhappiness. People with strong materialistic values are more anxious, more narcissistic, more depressed, use more mind altering substances, and have more relationship problems. They also tend to be more sedentary, sleep less, and tend to be emptier of heart and soul (Carver & Bard, 1998; Roberts & Robbins, 2000; Sagiv & Schwartz, 2000; Srivastava, Locke, & Bortol, 2001).

Not only does consumerism negatively influence personal happiness, it has a profound impact on the social structures of society. In the US, for instance, the period between 1960 and 1995 was a time of soaring economic vitality. The market was up but the social fabric was sinking. Americans are better paid, better fed, better housed, better educated, and have more conveniences than ever and yet in the 35 year period beginning in 1960, American society has seen profound social indices of decline (Frank, 1999; Inglehart, 1990; Myers, 2000; Suzuki, 1997). For example, since 1960:

- The teen suicide rate has tripled
- The divorce rate has doubled
- The violent crime rate has quadrupled
- The prison population has quintupled
- The number of children born to unmarried parents has sextupled
- Co-habitation has increased sevenfold
- Depression has increased ten times from pre World-War II levels
- More American are overweight or obese than ever before, nearly two-thirds of the population
- Parents spend 40% less time with their children than in 1960
- Employees work over five weeks longer per year than in 1960 while spending fewer hours sleeping and fewer hours with friends
- The number of children under six on stimulant and antidepressant drugs has increased 580 percent

Never has a culture experienced more physical comfort combined with such emotional and social misery. Never have we felt freer or have our prisons overflowed to the breaking point. Never have we been so beseeched to enjoy pleasure, or more likely to suffer broken relationships. Never have we been more able to support positive global change or felt more vulnerable or threatened.

The death of earth systems

Not only is overconsumption a threat to the physical, emotional, and social health of humans, it is the single largest danger to the Earth's eco-systems. Nature is increasingly seen as fodder for the industrial fires of production and consumption. Earth systems are valued as infinite—as an inexhaustible resource base. Human beings, particularly in the global north, are consuming resources at a rate far outpacing the earth's ability to renew itself. Water, forests and clean air are being used or polluted at rates higher than can be sustained. Biodiversity is shrinking while the orgy of over-development goes on virtually unabated. The US consumes 25% of the world's energy while constituting only 5% of the world's population. Since 1940 Americans have used more mineral resources than all previous generation put together (Brown, 2001; Suzuki, 1997). In total, the industrial countries, comprising only one fourth of the world's population, consume 40-86 percent of the earth's various natural resources.

The statistics and factual data are sobering. Consumerism, beyond a certain minimal level, is damaging to individuals, societies, and the natural environment. The question is how to begin the change process? There are no simple answers. And yet, there is a new social renewal and sustainable development movement underway. This movement has grassroots origins and is trickling upward from far-flung areas of the world, where wealth and consumption may be low but where happiness and community pride are still relatively high. And, just below the surface of the quiet desperation of industrial peoples is a perception that something in the modern ethos needs to change.

People across the globe are looking for a new story to define who they are and where they want to go (Besthorn, 2002a). Instead of one narrowly focused on material progress, they want a more coherent vision that expresses a better balance between economics, social equity, and environmental sustainability—a vision where these factors are inextricably linked. Unfortunately, too many national and international policy responses to the crisis of consumerism still reflect the current paradigm in which they are framed. Thus, reordering of the consumer world requires a radical change in the worldview of consumer societies and the individuals which inhabit them. As for social work as a profession, I am proposing that we consider alternative conceptualizations of social justice if we are to truly play a meaningful role in this transformation.

Consumer culture and social justice

Current conceptualization of social justice

Until very recently social work has generally viewed consumer culture and social justice as related only peripherally. That is, there has been a taken-for-granted and largely unexamined assumption that social justice exists within a worldview that generally accepts the underlying premises and some of the inevitable repercussions of consumer culture. The American profession has relied heavily on a Rawlsian model of justice whose main, although not sole, focus is the free and equitable distribution of available goods and services (Morris, 2002). The vehicle whereby this distribution, what Rawls (1971) calls *social primary goods,* takes place is through an increase in global material wealth by way of consumer production and spending practices. As Samuelson (1995, p.5) notes the central ambition of postwar conceptualizations of justice 'has been to create ever expanding prosperity at home and abroad ... because prosperity has seemed to be the path to higher goals'. These higher goals were inevitably concerned with social progress and included such laudable ambitions as the end to crime, slums and racial injustices. It has been, and still is, ardently believed that increasing global prosperity through the production of, demand for and usage of consumer products will in the end alleviate poverty, spread democracy, and insure social and economic justice.

It is, however, futile for us not to appreciate the finely nuanced connection between globalized consumerism and the hoped for equitable distribution of primary goods. The sobering reality is that as the popular desire to possess and consume more and more accelerates, both in the global north and south, it is becoming increasingly apparent this *never ending progress at any cost* is at the root of rising social injustice rather than its opposite (Mayer, 1998). Even as overall wealth continues to increase in the western world, there is strong evidence of declining social welfare for large segments of society in both the developed, but especially, the developing world. Indeed, huge gaps exist between the promise of consumer culture and its reality. As Athanasiou (1996) notes in his perceptive work *Divided Planet: The Ecology of Rich and Poor,* the relative wealth of rich and poor nations has begun to change rapidly over the last thirty years. This change, largely attributable to a virulent form of predatory capitalism and rapacious consumerism, has become an ultimately end in itself and accrues its benefits disproportionately upon those countries with greater political and economic power. He notes that this has not always been the case. From 1750, when standards of living for citizens in the global north were only marginally higher than for those in the global south,

The *average citizen* of the capitalist world grew to be eight times richer than one in the non-capitalist world, and contrary to all the tales told by friends of *progress*, this *improvement* has not always been by virtue of the North's technological and cultural innovations. The less-flattering and, according to Robert Heilbroner (1993, p.55-56), *more important* side of the story, 'was the drainage of wealth from the underdeveloped periphery to the developed Center—a capitalist version of the much-older imperialist exploitation of the weak by the strong.' (pp.53-54)

In the final analysis 'consumption has become an end in itself, rather than a means to individual enlightenment or happiness, or as a means to social justice, either domestically or globally' (Mayer, 1998, p.70).

Alternative conceptualization: A capabilities perspective

It often appears to us and we have been told repeatedly that there is no alternative to the global religion of secular salvation through international markets of conspicuous consumption. And yet, many noted social critics, economists, political scientists and proponents from a vast array of non-governmental organization have been saying for decades that curbing overconsumption and moving toward a more sustainable and socially just economy is not only possible but is absolutely necessary if the world community is to avoid catastrophic environmental and social upheaval and find ways to live in harmony (Besthorn, 2000, 2001, 2002, 2002a; Besthorn & Canda, 2002; Besthorn & Saleebey, 2004; Eckersley, 1998, 1999; International Institute for Environment and Development, 1998; Kasser, 2002; Michaelis, 2000; Myers, 2000; United Nations Commission on Sustainable Development, 1999; United Nations Human Development Programme, 1998; World Commission on Environment and Development, 1987). The earth's carrying capacity simply cannot support an American-made style of gargantuan consumptive excess. If every nation in the world were to consume at the US level it would require six earths to support such a rapacious pattern of consumption (Brown, 2001).

The emerging international consensus, although far from being fully articulated, has a number of broad parameters. In the short term, it recognizes that advocating a slowed economic agenda that places priority on *relative material equality* is critical. Until societies can agree to a new collective vision of the good life, the idea of relative material equality through more traditional consumptive practices offers an important but limited corrective to the demand for more material possessions. In the short term, if relative material equality becomes a global, social priority then the incessant process of achieving higher privilege through ever increasing accumulation of material possessions would be diminished though not totally eliminated.

Ultimately, however, initiatives toward a revised agenda of global social and economic action must go beyond an equitable redistribution of material resources as traditional models of social justice posit. A radical world political transformation of consciousness and actions has become necessary (WCED, 1987). At the heart of this new agenda is a new view of what constitutes a satisfying versus a satiated life. It is vision that seeks ways to live compatibly with a natural environment that can support the continuation of human life and well-being. It must reflect a long-term commitment to identifying sources of human satisfaction that can intergenerationally flourish in harmony with nature. The focus of human satisfaction changes from the quantity of life's possessions to the quality of life.

The Capabilities Approach, first pioneered by Harvard economist and Nobel Prize laureate Amartya Sen (1985, 1992), offers an alternative model of a socially just and fulfilling life that is not singularly dependent on quantity of life's possessions for its ontological grounding. The perspective defines well-being in terms of experiencing non-material capabilities rather than distribution of material goods. Well-being refers to unique ways in which individuals find value in their social functioning and achievement and how these are supported within their respective communities. The emphasis shifts radically from *human having* to *human being*, from material accumulation equaling happiness to quality of life capabilities as a significant contributor to well being.

As contemporary social work theorist Patricia McGrath Morris (2002, p. 368) notes:

> in contrast to the Rawlsian institutional framework that defines society's social justice principles, the capabilities approach examines the conception of what makes a good life for an individual and builds on this to develop the capabilities framework for a just society.

A significant shift of consciousness will not be an easy undertaking, especially for most Western societies, for many have lost the language and facility to assess satisfaction apart from material consumption. A capabilities social justice agenda can contribute to a new view of human satisfaction by helping people appraise ways of being that are internally rewarding, fully sustainable, not damaging to nature and not based on consumptive materialism. Important activities would include such simple activities as plain conversation, civic participation, spiritual rituals, neighborhood/community gatherings, family outings, artistic pursuits, music, dance, literature, and experiencing nature. This is a kind of sustainable life vision adorned with nonmaterial sources of fulfillment. It includes the kinds of activities and associations which most people affirm are the main determinants of happiness (Durning, 1992, 1996).

Nussbaum (1999, 2000) has built extensively on Sen's work and offers a more finely nuanced conceptualization of a socially just society from a capabilities perspective. Like Sen, Nussbaum argues that social justice, properly conceived, includes more than just a fair distribution of available goods or the freedom to pursue one's dedicated interests without interference. For Nussbaum, a socially just society ensures a safety net of core capabilities that allows each person to live a fully human life filled with opportunities to actualize one's internal and external potential within a supportive environmental context. This perspective does not adopt a kind of neo-Luddite escapism eschewing all material advances but rather shifts the uncritical focus away from material accumulation to the achievement of an inter-generationally sustainable life style festooned with predominately nonmaterial sources of well-being. It offers to extend our understanding of social justice beyond meeting some minimal level of material need. It accentuates social work's historic emphasis on the inherent dignity and well-being of persons in their unique space. Again Morris (2002) perceptively observes:

Similar to social work's perspective of person-in-environment, Nussbaum's central capabilities are comprised of what she calls 'combined capabilities'—capabilities that require both internal and external states of readiness. She asserts that to realize a central capability 'entails not only promoting the appropriated development of people's internal powers, but also preparing the environment' to secure the capability to achieve well-being. (p.369)

Nussbaum has developed a set of ten central capabilities critical to living a fully human life in a manner not heavily dependent upon traditional neo-liberal admonitions suggesting self worth comes most readily as a by-product of amassing material goods. These core capabilities extend far beyond a redistribution of primary goods and focus on central, generally nonmaterial, qualities necessary to a just and sustainable society. The ultimate measure of living fully human lives is how well we live rather than how long. The following table is an adaptation of Morris's (2002) review of Nussbaum's (2000) original work. The current conceptualization adds two additional factors called family/community and sustainability.

Life/well-being

Being able to live well to the end of a human life of normal length

Bodily Health

Being able to have good health, including reproductive health, to be adequately nourished; to have adequate shelter and sanitation facilities

Bodily Integrity

Being able to move freely from place to place; having one's bodily boundaries treated as sovereign; to be able to honor the sensate faculties of the body to experience its world

Senses, thought, imagination and spirituality

Being able to use the senses to imagine, think, reason and intuit—and to do these things in a truly human way....Being able to use imagination and thought in connection with experiencing and producing self-expressive works of creativity and functions of one's own choice, religious, spiritual literary, musical and so forth. Being able to use one's creative capacities in ways protected by guarantees of freedom of expression.

Connectivity Emotions

Being able to have attachments to things, humans and non-human beings outside ourselves. Not having one's emotional development blighted by overwhelming fear and anxiety, consumeristic induced sense of scarcity, or by traumatic events of war, abuse or neglect.

Practical and Moral reasoning

Being able to form a conception of the good and to engage in critical reflection about the planning of one's life

Affiliation

Being able to live with and toward other human and non-human others, to recognize and show as a dignified being whose worth is equal to that of others.

Other species

Being able to live with concern for and in relation to animal, plants, and the world of nature.

Play/recreation

Being able to laugh, to play, and to enjoy recreational activities.

Interaction with one's social and physical environment

Being able to participate effectively in socio-political choices that govern one's life, being able to hold property in conjunction with the common good; having the right to seek employment on an equal basis with others; and having the freedom from unwarranted intrusions into one's personal life by governmental or corporate interests.

Family/Community

Being able to live safely and without fear of want or privation within family structures that enhance individual development and communal connection. Being able to establish, maintain and choose local communities of support that are mutually fulfilling and which contribute to individual well-being and collective cohesiveness

Sustainability

Meeting the needs of present and future generations for goods, services and support that are economically, socially and environmentally sustainable.

These capabilities become a primary epistemological starting point for social work to enrich its instructional and practice frameworks. Although embryonic, it offers the profession a meaningful framework to begin more refined critical reflection on its historic social justice efforts.

Implications for social work and practice teaching

The question our previous discussion elicits is how this impacts the teaching of social work practice. One may reasonably ask, what does all this have to do with the typical social work academic or practice instructor in the classroom or in the field trying very hard to inculcate ideas of self-determination, service and social justice into their doe-eyed students. At the level of micro practice, if social work is to live conscientiously out of its commitment to and value for social justice it must face square on it's tacit approval of a model of society that creates ever deeper inequality and environmental degradation—insuring a world hell-bent on racing to its inevitable end.

Consumer capitalism makes profit out of the disappointment and depression of the unsatisfied masses. The rage and alienation engendered by unreal and unhealthy social comparisons, overheated aspirations and inflated guarantees promising more than can ever be delivered is a significant contributory cause, , for a spiraling array of mental health and social problems in many parts of the world. As professionals, we must ask, how are we serving the best interests, dignity and justice interests of our clients by suggesting that the key to their healing and progress is to join this march to madness? Indeed, by virtue of their poverty, ethnicity or class many of the people social worker's serve already feel lost and depressed because of their lack of access to this system—by their failure to live up to a kind of spurious individualism that defines self through purchases and possessions. Are we simply suggesting that our clients find a way, with our help, to do 'the system' better?

Social work can never just be about pandering to the interests of the elite, ruling class by serving up consumer oriented, western style homilies on family values, moral breakdown, hard work and consumer nirvana to the struggling masses in western society and the desolate poor of the developing world. Social work must begin to seriously reconsider a model of justice advocating for a solution that simply posits a more equitable and fair distribution of material resources. If we do not, we are simply finding more creative ways to encourage our clients to full participation in a culture of desire that increasingly conditions them to detest who they are, to resent how they look, to covet what they don't have and to relentlessly endeavor to meet their perceived failures through bigger or better artifacts of consumer society. The absolute critical psycho-social component to consumer capitalism is to first make us miserable and then to promise us our salvation through some item for consumption which will cure our misery. Many of our clients know this story all to well and know how utterly impossible it is to keep pace with it.

Practice teaching in the United States is commonly referred to as field education or field work. It has historically played a pivotal role in the profession's development and is one of the unique markers of social work. It is where students get their first real taste of the rigors of practice. One of most identifiable impacts of a globalized culture is the degree to which public service institutions have been eclipsed by a new emphasis on a competitive, private, consumeristic, marketplace mentality. Clients are no longer clients—they have become consumers.

The potentially disastrous impact of this fundamental shift in service ideology on practice teaching specifically and social work education generally in the US is beginning to find its way into the literature (Besthorn, 2004; Donner, 1996; Emenhiser, Barker, & DeWoody, 1995; Evans, 1999; Fisher & Karger, 1997; Gibelman & Demone, 1998; Regehr, Leeson, Regehr & Fusco, 2002). No attempt will be made to elucidate those findings here. Rather, our purpose shall be to consider a number of important first principles that have emerged from a reconsideration of globalized consumer culture impact on social work's social justice and practice teaching legacies.

First, the profession must begin to incorporate insights from alternative theoretical models into a much richer and more complex worldview than that provided by traditional, neo-liberal, social welfare based economism. Social workers are world citizens first and foremost, not only having a responsibility to train students in professional knowledge and technique, but also to help catalyze a conscientization of responsibility to a world community which can only survive in a culture of permanence and peace. Secondly, social work must develop a much more sophisticated understanding of the relationship of consumerism to meeting basic human needs. What is the purpose of consumerism as currently conceived and how does it contribute to actually meeting basic human needs and improving quality of life? At a minimum, this analysis would suggest, thirdly, that we begin the difficult dialogue of appraising the ethics of a globalized consumer culture and the uncritical linkage of it with human well-being and core tenets of social work practice. Initial questions would involve assessing how one person's consumptive patterns prevents others from meeting their most basic needs, how consumerism inhibits full social participation, how and to what degree does consumerism contribute to human happiness and in what way is the earth's carrying capacity seriously strained by unfettered material accumulation. Fourth, social work must explore the meaning of each of the twelve core components of the Capabilities Perspective which we have suggested as essential for living a fully human life. We must also consider their applicability to social work's understanding of a just society and how the profession has tended to define the good life, well-being, happiness and success. The global Eco-Village Movement (Trainer, 1998), now emerging in parts of Europe, North America and the developing world, is just one example of a movement that is grabbling with these concerns in everyday reality and is a place social work can learn from and contribute to a sustainable, post-consumeristic society.

Finally, the profession must develop new ways to train future social workers through our practice teaching protocols. This means finding innovative means to educate social workers who will *not* simply work to maintain the status quo—working to shape our clients into better *producers* and *consumers*. This suggests a profession sensitized to the difference between *working with* versus *helping* clients. In a sense, social workers are more than just social workers. We are human workers, who walk beside, witness, encourage, and support the capacity of every human being *to live a fully human life.* As this quote from an anonymous aboriginal woman proffers,

> if you have come to help us, you are wasting your time. But if you have come because your liberation is bound up with ours, then let us work together. (Sheridan, personal communication)

Conclusion

This chapter has suggested that we are at a critical apex of history. By most accounts, this is a very difficult transition moment in human evolution. New vision is required. In the words of Ramonet (1998, p. 1) 'there is a need for dreamers who can think and thinkers who can dream. The answer will not be a neatly-packaged, custom-built project. It will be a new way of looking at things.' In like manner, social work needs a new vision of globalization, a revised definition of social justice and creative new ways to help enhance the capacity of all human beings while steadfastly sustaining the earth. We can continue with our current ideology of consumerism and continue blindly down the path of high material accumulation accompanied by diminishing happiness, greater social stratification and increased eco-system devastation. Or, we can come together with an emerging collective consciousness and aspire to a new ascension that is grounded in sound policy, enlivened by a new commitment and inspired by a greater faith. As Myers (2000) suggests:

> This ascension is similar to climbing to the next anthropological stage. No one on earth has any other way left—but upward...Those who take this upward road—those who live remembering the future—will fulfill the ancient prophecy ... 'You shall raise up the foundations of many generations; you shall be called the repairer of the breach, the restorer of streets to live in'. (p.295)

The choice and the action to birth a new world based on

capabilities rather than consumption is ours. Admittedly, given the current state of human affairs this vision seems a long way from coming to fruition. But, in light of the remarkable potential emerging in the human species, it is hard to imagine a possibility more worthy of our collective imagination and inspiration.

References

Abdalla, M. (2002) 'Attitude of first year medical and dentistry students towards problem based learning'. University of Gezira, Sudan, Network-TUFH conference, Eldoret, Kenya, September 7-12.

Advisory Committee on SWT & Manpower Planning: Review of Role of Social Work Training Provides on the Training & Development for Social Workers in an Era of Change (Draft) October 2003

Akuffo, F.W.B., and Akuffo, M.S. (1989) 'The Role of youths in family development in Africa-The Zambia case'. In K. Osei-Hwedie and N. Ndulo (Eds.) *Studies in Youths in Family Development.* Lusaka: Multi-Media Publication

Alcock, P. (1997) *Understanding Poverty.* (2nd ed.) Basingstoke: Macmillan

Alcock, P. (2004) Participation or pathology: contradictory Tensions in area-based policy. *Social Policy and Society,* 3, 2, 87-96

Ali, E., Elgaili, D., Elhindi, Y. and Hassan, Y. (2002) 'Faculty of Applied Medical Sciences, University of Gezira, Sudan, meets the health services needs with multi professional education and partnership'. Network-TUFH conference, Eldoret, Kenya, September 7-12.

Alwan, A. and Hornby, P. (2002) The implications of health sector reform for human resources development. *Bulletin of the World Health Organization,* 80, 1, 56-60.

Aristotle (1948) *Politics* (translated and edited by E. Barker) Oxford: Clarendon Press

Arkin, N. (1999) A group supervision model for broadening multiple-method skills of social work students. *Social Work Education,* 19, 1

Asante, M.K., (2002) Forward to M.Graham, *Social Work and African Centered World Views.* Birmingham: Venture Press.

Athanasiou, T. (1996) *Divided Planet: The ecology of rich and poor.* Toronto: Little Brown Press.

Australian Association of Social Workers (2000) *Code of Ethics.* Kingston. ACT: Australian Association of Social Workers.

Barnes, C. and Mercer, G. (2003) *Disability.* Cambridge: Polity Press

Barnes, C. Oliver, M. & Barton, M. (2002) *Disability Studies Today.* Cambridge: Polity Press

Barnett, R.A. (1992) *Improving Higher Education: Total Quality Care.* Buckingham: Society for research into higher Education / Open University Press

Barr, H., Freeth, D., Hammick, M., Koppel, I. and Reeves, S. (2000) *Evaluations of Interprofessional Education.* London: CAIPE/BERA.

Barr, H. (2002) *Interprofessional Education: Today, Yesterday and Tomorrow.* LTSN Occasional Paper No. 1. London: Learning and Teaching Support Network.

Barrows, H.S. and Tamblin, R.M. (1980) *Problem Based Learning.* New York: Springer Publications

Beresford, P (1994) *Changing the Culture: Involving service users in social work education.* CCETSW Paper 32.2. London: CCETSW

Beresford, P. and Holden, C. (2000) We have choices: Globalisation and welfare user movements. *Disability and Society,* 15, 7, 973-989

Berger, P. and Luckman, T. (1966) *The Social Construction of Reality.* Harmondsworth: Penguin

Besthorn, F.H. (2000) Toward a deep-ecological social work: Its environmental, spiritual and political dimensions. *The Spirituality and Social Work Forum,* 7, 2, 2-7.

Besthorn, F.H. (2001) Transpersonal psychology and deep ecological philosophy: Exploring linkages and applications for social work. *Social Thought,* 20, 1/2, 23-44.

Besthorn, F.H. (2002) Radical environmentalism and the ecological self: Rethinking the concept of self-identity for social work practice. *Journal of Progressive Human Services,* 13, 1, 53-72.

Besthorn, F.H. (2002a) Expanding spiritual diversity in social work: Perspectives on the greening of spirituality. Currents. *New Scholarship in the Human Services,* 1, 1. (Retrieved, November, 15, 2002, from http://fsw.ucalgary.ca/currents/fred_besthorn/besthorn.htm)

Besthorn, F. H. (2004) Globalization, privatization and the devolution of the social safety net: A US perspective on the implications for practice education. Manuscript submitted for publication to *Social Work Education: An International Journal.*

Besthorn, F.H. (2005) 'Hijacked by Fear: The War on Liberty and the Future of Social Work' Paper presented as keynote speech at the 4th International Conference for the Journal of Practice Teaching in Health and Social Work, York, 4/5 July 2005

Besthorn, F.H. & Canda, E.R. (2002) Revisioning environment: Deep ecology for education and teaching in social work. *Journal of Teaching in Social Work,* 22, 1/2, 79-102.

Besthorn, F.H. & McMillen, D. (2002) Re-shaping American social services delivery for a new millennium. *Journal of Practice Teaching in Health and Social Work*, 4, 2, 28-47

Besthorn, F.H. & Saleebey D. (2004) Nature, genetics, and the biophilia connection: Exploring linkages with social work values and practice. *Advances in Social Work*, 4. 1. 1-18.

Bond, M.H. & King, Ambrose Y.C. (1985) Coping with the Treat of Westernization in Hong Kong., *International Journal of Intercultural Relations*, 9

Bond, M.H. (1991) Beyond the Chinese Face: Insights from psychology. Hong Kong: Oxford University Press.

Boyden, J & Ennew, J. (Eds.) (1997) *Children in Focus: A manual for participatory research with children*. Stockholm: Radda Barnen [quoted in Cavet, J. and Sloper, P. (2003) *The Participation of Children and Young People in UK Service Development*,. York: University of York, Social Policy Research Unit]

British Association of Social Workers (2002) *The code of Ethics for Social Workers*. Birmingham: BASW

Bridge, G. (2000) Let's develop practice learning in Eastern Europe: Innovation in Ukraine and Armenia. *Journal of Practice Teaching in Heath and Social Work*, 2. 3, 47-60

Brigham, T.M. (1974) *Liberation in Social Work Education: Applications from Paulo Freire*. Paper from School of Social Work. California State University. Frenso

BRTF (2004) *Bridging the Gap: Participation in social care regulation*. London: Cabinet Office, Better Regulation Taskforce

Brown, L.R. (2001) *Eco-economy: Building an economy for the earth*. New York: W. W. Norton.

Brubaker, W.S.R. (1992) *Citizenship and Nationhood in France and Germany*. Cambridge, MA: Harvard University Press

Campbell, J. and McColgan, M. (2002) *Social Work in the British Isles.London:* Jessica Kingsley.

Campbell, J. and Pinkerton, J. (1998) Social Work, social conflict and social change in Northern Ireland: Learning from international comparisons, in challenge and change. *International Social Work*, 45, 2, 217-238.

Carageta, L. and Sanchez, M. (2002) (Eds.) *Globalisation and Global Need*. Sage, London.

Carroll, M. (1986) The carrier role of social work: Learning from Alaskan Native Americans. *Social Casework,* 67, 3, 180-184.

Carver, C.S., & Bard, E. (1998) The American dream revisited: Is it what you want or why you want it that matters? *Psychological Science*, 9, 289-292.

CCETSW (1996) *Assuring Quality 1. Rules and regulations for the Diploma in Social Work.* (revised edition) London: CCETSW

Cederborg, A., Orbach, Y., Sternberg K.J., & Lamb M. E. (2000) Investigative interviews of child witnesses in Sweden. *Child Abuse & Neglect*, 24, 10, 1355-1361.

Celebrating Good Practice in Social Work in Northern Ireland. BASW.

Chan, K.L. (1980) Notes on Chinese culture. in P. Hodge (Ed.) *Culture & Social Work Education & Practice in Southeast Asia.* London: Heinemann

Chan, K.L. (1995) Social work practice in a Chinese society: Reflections and challenges, *Hong Kong Journal of Social Work*, 2, 2-10

Chan Wing-tsit (1967) *The Story of Chinese Philosophy*. Honolulu: East West Center Press / University of Hawaii Press.

Chilbuye, P.S., Mwenda, M. and Osborn, L. (1986) *Study on Child Rearing Practices in Zambia.* Lusaka: GRZ/UNICEF

Chomsky, N. (2003) *Middle East Illusions.* Oxford: Rowan and Littlefield

Christopher, J. C. (1996) Counseling's inescapable moral visions. *Journal of Counseling and Development*, 75, 17-25.

Cockburn, T. (2005) Children's participation in social policy: inclusion, chimera or authenticity? *Social Policy and Society*, 4, 2, 109-119

Chow, N. (1997) China in N.S. Mayadas, T.D. Watts, D. Elliott (1997) *International Handbook on Social Work Theory and Practice.* Westport, CT: Greenwood Press

Collins Dictionary 21st Edition.

Contact a Family (2004) *Parent Participation: Improving services for disabled children, a professional guide.* London: Contact a Family and Council fro Disabled Children

Cornwell, A., Haroutanian, M., Muradian, S. and Rachman, C (1999) Social work education in a transitional country: issues and dilemmas. *Issues in Social Work Education*, 19, 2, 46-55

Cremins, R.S. (1984) *What Kind of Family Life Education for our Children?* Lusaka: Family Life Movement in Zambia (FLMZ) Mimeo

Crocker, D. A., & Linden, T. (Eds.) (1998) *Ethics of Consumption: The good life, justice, and global stewardship.* New York: Rowman & Littlefield Publishers.

Davys, A. and Beddoe, L. (2000) Supervision of students: A map and a model for the decade to come, *Social Work Education*, 19, 5, 437- 449

Department of Health (2002) *Requirements for Social Work Training.* London:

Department of Health.

DoH (2002) *Requirements of Social Work Training,* London: Department of Health

DoH (2004) *The National Forensic Mental Health Research and Development Programme.* London: Department of Health

Diaz-Lazaro, C.M., and Cohen, B.B. (2001) Cross-cultural contact in counselor training. *Journal of Multicultural Counseling and Development,* 29, 1, 41-56.

Diener, E., & Oishi, S. (2000) Money and happiness: Income and subjective well-being across nations. in E. Diener & E. M. Suh (Eds.) *Subjective Well-being Across Cultures.* Cambridge, MA: The MIT Press

Dillon, J. T. (1990) *The Practice of Questioning.* New York : Routledge

Doel, M. & Shardlow, S. (2005) *Modern Social Work Practice.* Aldershot: Ashgate

Doel, M. and Sawdon, C. (1999) *The Essential Groupworker: Teaching and learning creative groupwork.* London: Jessica Kingsley

Doel, M, Shardlow, S., Sawdon, C. and Sawdon, D. (1996) *Teaching Social Work Practice: a programme of exercises and activities towards the Practice Teaching Award.* Aldershot: Arena

Dominelli, L. and Hoogvelt, A. (1996) *Critical Social Policy,* 16., 45-62

Donner, S. (1996) Field work crisis: Dilemmas, dangers, and opportunities. *Smith College Studies in Social Work,* 66, 317-331.

Dominelli, L. (1988) *Anti-racist Social Work: A challenge for white practitioners and educators.* Basingstoke, Macmillan

Durning A. (1992) *How Much is Enough?* New York: W.W. Norton.

Durning, A. (1996) *This Place on Earth: Home and the practice of permanence.* Seattle: Sasquatch Books.

Dwyer, P. (2004) *Understanding Social Citizenship.* Bristol: Polity Press

Eckersley, R. (1998) Perspectives on progress: Economic growth, quality of life and ecological sustainability. In R. Eckersley, (Ed.) *Measuring Progress: Is life getting better?* Collingwood, AU: CSIRO Publishing.

Eckersley, R. (1999) Measuring well-being: Material progress and quality of life. Paper presented at the Council of Social Service, Sydney, NSW, Australia.

Cohen, L.A. (2003) *Consumers' Republic: The politics of mass consumption in postwar America.* New York: Alfred A. Knopf.

Emenhiser, D. L., Barker, R. L., & DeWoody, M. (1995) *Managed Care: An agency guide to survival and thriving.* Washington, D.C.: Child Welfare League of America.

Eraut, M., Alderton, J., Cole, G., Senker, P. (2000) 'Development of knowledge and skills at work. in F. Coffield, *Differing visions of a Learning Society: Research findings. Volume 1.* Bristol: The Policy Press

Eraut, M. (1997) Curriculum frameworks and assumptions in 14-19 education. *Research in Post-Compulsory Education,* 2, 3.

Evans, D. (1999) *Practice Learning in the Caring Professions.* Aldershot, UK: Ashgate.

Faure, D. (2003) *Colonialism & the Hong Kong Mentality.* Hong Kong: University of Hong Kong

Fie, X.T. (1992) *From the Soil: The foundations of Chinese society.* (Translated from Fei Xiaotong *Xiangtu Zhongguo*) Berkeley, CA: University of California Press

Fisher, R., & Karger, H.J. (1997) *Social work and Community in a Private World: Getting out in public.* New York: Longman.

Ford, K. and Jones, A. (1984) *Student Supervision.* London: Macmillian.

Forman, D. and Nyatanga, L. (1999) The Evolution of shared Learning: some political and professional imperatives. *Medical Teacher,* 21, 489-496

Francis, L.K. Hsu (1968) Chinese kinship and Chinese behavior. in Ho Ping-ti & Tsou Tang (Eds.) *China in Crisis, Vol. one, Book Two, Chinese Heritage and the Communist Political System.* Chicago: University of Chicago Press.

Frank, R.H. (1999) *Luxury Fever: Money and happiness in an era of excess.* New York: The Free Press.

Frederickson, H.G. and Schluter O'Leary, L. (1973) *Power, Public Opinion and Policy in a Metropolitan Community: A case study of Syracuse, New York.* New York: Praeger.

Freeth, D., Meyer, J., Reeves, S. and Spilsbury, K. (1999) Linking interprofessional education to user benefit: Of drops in the ocean and stalactites. *Advanced Clinical Nursing,* 3, 366-372.

Freire, P. (1972) *Pedagogy of the Oppressed.* London: Penguin.

Fukuyama, F. (1995) *Trust: The social virtues and the creation of prosperity.* New York: Free Press.

Funnell, P. (1995) Exploring the value of interprofessional shared learning. In: K. Soothill, I. McKay And C. Webb *Interprofessional Relations in Health Care.* London: Edward Arnold.

Geertz, C. (1973) *The Interpretations of Cultures.* New York: Basic Books.

General Social Care Council (2002) *Codes of Practice for Social Care Workers and Employers.* London: GSCC

Gibelman, M. & Demone, H. W. (1998) *The Privatization of Human Services: Policy and practice issues.* New York: Springer.

References

Gold, S. (2002) *The Israeli Diaspora*. London: Routledge.

Gonzalez, R. C. (1997) Postmodern supervision: A multicultural perspective. in D.B. Pope-Davis and H.L.K. Coleman (Eds.) *Multicultural Counseling Competencies: Assessment, education and training and supervision*. Thousand Oaks, CA. Sage.

Goldberg, M. (2000) Conflicting principles in multicultural social work. *Families in Society*, 8, 12-21.

Goodwin, N. R., Ackerman, F., & Kiron, D. (Eds.) (1997) *The Consumer Society*. Washington, DC: Island Press.

Graham, M. (2002) *Social Work and African Centered World Views*. Birmingham: Venture Press

Guzzetta, C. (1990) 'Introduction to L. Carageta and M. Sanchez, *Globalisation and Global Need*. London: Sage.

Hagshama, (1998) Department of the World Zionist Organisation. Submitted by the publications department, Ministry of Immigrant Absorption: department of Aliyah and Absorption of the Jewish Agency-Social Workers.

Hamad, B. (1982) Interdisciplinary Field Training Research and Rural Development Programme. *Medical Education*, 16,105-107.

Hargadon, J. and Staniforth, M. (2000) *A Health Service of All the Talents: Developing the NHS workforce*. London: Department of Health

Harris, N. (1998) *Israel and the Arab Nations in Conflict*. Hove: Wayland.

Harrison, L.E. (1985) *Underdevelopment is a State of Mind: The Latin American case*. Lanham, Md: Madison Books.

Harrison, L.E. (1992) *Who Prospers? How cultural values shape economic and political success*. New York: Basic

Harrison, L.E. (1997) *The Pan American Dream: Do Latin American's cultural values discourage true partnership?* New York: Basic

Healy, L. (1990) International curriculum content: The Challenge of Relevance for Social Work. in K. Kendall (Ed.) *The International in American Education*. New York.

Heilbroner, R. (1993) *Twenty First Century Capitalism*. New York: W.W. Norton.

Inglehart, R. (1990) *Culture Shift in Advanced Industrial Society*. Princeton, NJ. Princeton University Press.

Hewitt, M. (1999) New Labour and social security. in M. Powell (Ed.) *New Labour New Welfare State? The third way in British social policy*. Bristol: The Policy press

Highlen, P. S. (1996) MCT theory and implications for organizations/systems. in D.W. Sue, A.E. Ivey, and P.B. Pedersen (Eds.) *A Theory Of*

Multicultural Counselling And Therapy. Pacific Grove, CA, Brooks/Cole.

Ho, M.K. (1992) *Minority Children and Adolescents in Therapy.* Newbury Park, CA. Sage.

Ho, D.Y.F. (1989) Therapeutic intervention for parents and children in Hong Kong problem, Frustrations and reflections from a cross cultural perspective. Hong Kong Journal of Social Work, 13, 1, 15-22.

Hodge, P. (1980) *Social work education. In P. Hodge (Ed.) Community Problems and Social Work in Southeast Asia: The Hong Kong and Singapore experience.* Hong Kong: Hong Kong University Press

HMSO. (2000) *Care Standards Act 2000,* London: HMSO

Hokenstad, C. et al, (1992) *Social Work Today and Tomorrow. An International Perspective.* Washington, DC: NASW Press

Huntingdon, S.P. (1996) *The Clash of Civilisation and the Remaking of World Order.* New York: Simon and Schuster

Huston, S. and Campbell, J. (2001) Using critical social theory to develop a conceptual framework for comparative social work. *International Journal of Social Work,* 10, 66-73.

Inglehart, R. (1990) *Culture Shift in Advance Industrial Society.* Princeton: Princeton University Press.

Inglehart, R. (1997) *Modernization and Post-modernization Cultural, Economic and Political Change in Forty-Three Societies.* Princeton: Princeton University Press

Inglehart, R. (2000) Culture and democracy. in L. Harrison and S. Huntingdon (Eds.) *Culture Matters: How values shape human progress.* New York: Basic

International Institute for Environment and Development, (1998) *Consumption in a Sustainable World: Report of the workshop held in Kabelvag, Norway.* Oslo, Norway: Ministry of the Environment.

Ivey, A.E. (1987) Reaction: Cultural intentionality: The core of effective helping. *Counselor Education and Supervision,* 26, 168-172.

Ivey, A.E. , Ivey, M.B., and Simek-Morgan, L. (1997) *Counseling and Psychotherapy: A multicultural perspective.* Needham Heights, MA, Allyn and Bacon.

Ivey, A.E., Pedersen, P.B. and Ivey, M.B. (2001) *Intentional Group Counseling: A microskills approach.* Belmont, CA, Wadsworth.

Johnson, P. ((1989) Cross-cultural casework with the Indo-Chinese. Conference Proceedings, Australian Association of Social Workers Conference, Townsville, August, 36-38.

Kasser, T. (2002) *The high Price of Materialism.* Cambridge, MA: MIT Press.

Keefe, T. (2004) *Wild Man.* Unpublished manuscript.

Khanna, S., & Kasser, T. (2001) *Materialism, Objectification, And Alienation From A Cross-cultural Perspective.* Cambridge, MA: MIT Press.

Knowles, M. (1980) *The Modern Practice of Adult Education: From pedagogy to androgogy.* New York: Association Press.

Kolb, D. (1984) *Experiential Learning.* New Jersey: Prentice Hall

Kolb, D and Fry, R. (1975) 'Toward an applied theory of experimental learning. in C. Cooper (Ed.) *Theories of Group Process.* London: John Wiley.

Kwong, W.M. (1996) Local knowledge, indigenous practice: Linking the cultural, the personal, and the professional in social work practice. *Hong Kong Journal of Social Work,* 33, 1, 22-30.

Labov, W & Fanshell, D. (1977) *Therapeutic Discourse.* New York: Academic Press.

Lane, R. (2000) *The Loss of Happiness in Market Democracies.* New Haven, CT: Yale University Press

Lassiter, J.E.(1999) African culture and personality: Bad social science, effective social activism, or a call to reinvent? *Ethnology,* 3, 2, 1. [online] http://web.africa.ufl.edu/asq/v3/v3i2a1.htm

Layer, D. (1997) *Modern Social Theory, Key Debates and New Directions.* London: UCL Press

Levitas, R. (1998) *The Inclusive Society? Social exclusion and New Labour.* Basingstoke: Macmillan

LFPN (2003) International and global issues affecting the development and learning of Interprofessional Education. A discussion paper by Graham Ixer, General Social Care Council given at the Learning for Partnership Network, 23 June 2003, London

Lister, R. (2003) Citizenship and gender. in K. Nash & A. Scott (Eds) *The Blackwell companion to Political Sociology.* Oxford: Blackwell

Lorenz, W. (1994) *Social Work in a Changing Europe.* London: Routledge

Loughlan, C. (2003/4) The NHSU Learning Needs Observatory. *Eurohealth,* 9, 4, 33-37

Lyons, K. (2000) *International Social Work: Themes and perspectives.* Aldershot: Ashgate.

Mak, D. & Tsang, N.M. (1997) Social work education in context: Hong Kong Polytechnic File in D. Tucker, R. Garvin, and R. Sarri (Eds.) *Integrating Knowledge and Practice: The Case of Social Work & Social Science.* Westport, CT: Praeger

Marshall, T.H. and Bottonmore, T. (1992) *Citizenship and Social Class.* London: Pluto Press

Mayadas, N.S., Watts, T.D., Elliott, D. (1997) *International Handbook on Social Work Theory and Practice*. Westport, CT: Greenwood Press

Mayer, D. (1998) Institutionalizing over consumption. In L. Westra & P. H. Werhane (Eds.) *The business of Consumption: Environmental ethics and the global economy*. New York: Rowan & Littlefield.

Mcleod, J. (1998) *An Introduction to Counselling*. 2nd edition. Buckingham: Open University Press

Meads, G., Griffiths, F., Wild, A. Iwami, M., Arroyo Laguna, J., Montero, J. and Moore, P. (2005a) International lessons foe new organisational practice in primary care, *Seguridad Social Journal, 252*, 1-10.

Meads, G., Iwami, M. and Wild, A. (2005b) Transferable learning from international primary care developments. *International Journal of Health Planning and Management, 20, 3*, 253-267

Meads, G., Ashcroft, J., Barr, H., Scott, R. and Wild, A. (2005c) *The case for interprofessional Collaboration in Health and Social Care*. Oxford: Blackwells Science.

Michaelis, L. (2000) *Sustainable Consumption: A research agenda*. Oxford: The Oxford Centre for the Environment, Ethics and Society.

Midgely, J. (1990) International social work: learning from the Third World. *Social Work, 35, 4*, 295-301.

Milton-Edwards, B. and Hinchcliffe, P. (2004) *Conflicts in the Middle East since 1945*. 2nd Edition. London: Routledge.

Morris, P. M. (2002) The capabilities perspective: A framework for social justice. *Families in Society, 83, 4*, 265-273.

Morrison, T. (1993) *Staff Supervision in Social Care: An action learning approach*. Harlow: Longmans

Morton-Cooper, A. (2000) *Action research in Health Care*. Oxford: Blackwell Science.

Mukoboto, M. (1993) Early marriages: Zambia setting. Parenthood. 1, 14-15

Mur, I. and Van Raak, A. (2003) Integration of services and the European Union: Does EU policy make sense? International Journal of Integrated Care, 3, 1, 1-2

Myers, D. G. (2000) *The American Paradox: Spiritual hunger in an age of plenty*. New Haven, CT: Yale University Press.

Nagy, G. & Falk, D. (2000) Dilemmas in international and cross-cultural social work. *International Social Work*, Vol.43, 1, 49-60

National Organisation for Practice Teaching (2000) *Code of Practice for Practice Teachers*. Stockport: NOPT

Newman, J. Barnes, M. Sullivan, H. & Knops, A (2004) Public participation and collaborative governance. *Journal of Social Policy*, 33, 2, 203-23

Nguyen, T., and Bowles, R. (1998) Counselling Vietnamese refugee survivors of trauma: Points of entry for developing trust and rapport, *Australian Social Work,* 51, 2, 41-47.

NHS Confederation (2003) *Investing in General Practice. The New General Medical Services Contract.* London: Department of Health

NISCC (2003) *The Reform of Social Work Training. The Degree in Social Work in Northern Ireland.* Belfast: Northern Ireland Social Care Council.

Nozick, R. (1995) 'Distributive justice. in S. Avinri and A. de Shalit (Eds.) *Communitarism and Individualism.* Oxford: Oxford University Press

Nussbaum, M.C. (1999) Women and equality: The capabilities approach. *International Labor Review*, 138, 3, 227-251.

Nussbaum, M.C. (2000) *Women and Human Development: The capabilities approach.* Cambridge, MA: Cambridge University Press.

Nyasani, J.M. (1997) *The African Psyche.* Nairobi: University of Nairobi and Theological Printing Press

Pack-Brown, S.P. and Williams, C.B. (2000) To discriminate or not to discriminate: Culture and ethics. Counseling Today. Alexandria, VA: American Counseling Association.

Pack-Brown, S. P., Whittington-Clark, L. E., and Parker, W. M. (2002) *Images of Me: A guide to group work with African-American women.* Boston MA, Allyn and Bacon.

Pack-Brown, S. P. and Williams, C. B. (2003) *Ethics in a Multicultural Context.* Thousand Oaks, CA, Sage.

Paniagua, F. A. (1994) *Assessing and Treating Culturally Diverse Clients: A practical guide.* Thousand Oaks, CA., Sage.

Parker, J. & Paxton. W. (2005) *Social Justice: Building a fairer Britain.*London: Institute for Public and Policy Research

Payne, M. (1996) *What is Professional Social Work?* Venture Press.

Pedersen, P. B. (2000) *A Handbook For Developing Multicultural Awareness.* (3rd ed.) Alexandria, VA: American Counseling Association.

Pinkerton, J. (2002) *The RHP Companion to Leaving Care.* Lyme Regis: Russell House

Publications Department, (1996) English Section, Ministry of Immigrant Absorption 15 Rebhov Hillel, Jerusalem.

Punch, K. (2005) *Introduction to Social Research: Quantitative and qualitative approaches.* (2nd Edition) London: Sage

Race, P. (2001) *The Lecturer's Toolkit: A practical guide to learning, teaching and assessment.* London: Kogan Page

Ramonet, I (1998) There is another, better world: A need for utopia. *Le*

Monde Diplomatique, May, 1998 [Retrieved September, 14, 2003 at http://www.monde-diplomatique.tr/en/1998/05/17ramonet]

Ranger, T. (1993 The invention of tradition revisited: The case of colonial Africa. in T. Kanger and O. Vaughan (Eds.) *Legitimacy and the State in Twentieth-century Africa*. Basingstoke: Macmillian

Rawls, J. (1971) *A Theory of Justice*. Cambridge, MA: Harvard University Press.

Regehr, C., Leeson, J., Regehr, G. & Fusco, L. (2002) Setting priorities for learning in the field practicum; A comparative study of students and field instructors. *Journal of Social Work Education*, 38, 1, 55-65.

Richmond, M. (1917) *Social Diagnosis*. New York: Russell Sage Foundation.

Rimmer, A. (2005) What is professional social work? Social work and social justice. in S. Shardlow & M. Doel (Eds.) *Introducing Social Work*. Lyme Regis: Russell House

Roberts, B.W., & Robbins, R.W. (2000) Broad dispositions, broad aspirations: The intersection of personality traits and major life goals. *Personality and Social Psychology Bulletin,* 26, 1284-1296.

Robertson, R. *Globalisation. Social Theory and Global Culture.* London: Sage.

Robertson, D. and Dearling, A. (2004) *The Practical Guide to Social Welfare Research.* Lyme Regis: Russell House

Robson, P. Begum, N & Lock, M. (2003) *Increasing User Involvement in Voluntary Organisations.* York: Joseph Rowntree Foundation

Rogers, A. (1996) *Teaching Adults.* (2nd edition) Buckingham: Open University Press

Rogers, A. (2002) *Teaching Adults.* (3rd Edition) Maidenhead: Open University Press

Rosenblatt, R. (Ed.) (1999) *Consuming Desires: Consumption, culture, and the pursuit of happiness.* Washington, DC: Island Press.

Sagiv, L., & Schwartz, S. H. (2000) Value priorities and subjective well-being; Direct relations and congruity effects. *European Journal of Social Psychology*, 30, 177-198.

Samuelson, R. (1995) *The Good Life and its Discontents.* New York: Random House.

Saunder, S., & Munro, D. (2000) The construction and validation of a consumer orientation questionnaire (SCOI) designed to measure Fromm's 'marketing character' in Australia. *Social Behavior and Personality,* 28, 219-240

Scherpbier, A.J.J.A. (Chairman) (2001) *The New Maastricht Curriculum: Best*

Evidence-based medical education Maastricht: University of Maastricht, Blueprint New Curriculum Committee.

Schon, D. (1983) *The Reflective Practitioner: How professionals think in action.* New York, Basic Books.

SCIE (2003) *Users at the Heart: User participation in the governance and operations of social care regulatory bodies.* Report No.5, London: Social Care Institute for Excellence

SCIE (2004a) *Involving Service Users And Carers In Social Work Education.* Resource guide No. 2, London: Social Care Institute for Excellence

SCIE (2004b) *Has Service User Participation made a difference to Social Care services?* Position paper No.3, London: Social Care Institute for Excellence

Sen, A. (1985) *The Standard of Living: The Tanner Lectures.* Cambridge: Cambridge University Press.

Sen, A. (1992) *Inequality Re-examined.* New York: Russel Sage Foundation.

Srivastava, A., Locke, E.A., & Bortol, K.M. (2001) Money and subjective well-being: It's not the money, it's the motives. *Journal of Personality and Social Psychology,* 80, 559-571.

Sewpaul, V. & Jones, D (2004) Global standards for the education and training of the social work profession. *International Journal of Social Welfare,* 23, 5, 493-515

Shardlow, S. and Nelson, P. (2005) *Introducing Social Work.* Lyme Regis: Russel House publishing

Smith, E.J. (1981) Cultural and historical perspectives in counseling Blacks. in D.W. Sue (Ed.) *Counseling the Culturally Different: Theory and practice.* New York: John Wiley

SCIE (2003) *Users at the Heart: User participation in the governance and operations of social care regulatory bodies.* Report No.5. London: Social Care Institute for Excellence

Smyth, M. and Campbell, J. (1996) Social work, sectarianism, and anti sectarian practice in Northern Ireland. *British Journal of Social Work,* 26, 1, 77-92.

Sternberg, K.J. Lamb, M.E. Hershkowitz, I. Yudilevitch, L. Orbach, Y. Esplin, P.W. & Hovav, M. (1997) Effects of introductory style on children's abilities to describe experiences of sexual abuse. *Child Abuse & Neglect,* 21, 1133-1146.

Sue, D.W. and Sue, D. (1977) Barriers to effective cross-cultural counseling, *Journal of Counseling Psychology,* 24, 5, 420-429.

Sue, D. W., Ivey, A. E. and Pedersen, P. B. (1996) *A Theory of Multicultural*

Counseling and Therapy. Pacific Grove, CA, Brooks/Cole.

Sue, D.W., Carter, R.. T., Casas, J.M., Fouad, N A., Ivey, A.E., Jensen, M., LaFromboise, T., Manese, J.E., Ponterotto, J.G. and Vazquez-Nutall, E., (1998) *Multicultural Counseling Competencies.* Thousand Oaks, CA: Sage.

Sue, S. (1999) Science, ethnicity and bias: Where have we gone wrong? *American Psychologist,* 54, 2, 1070-1077.

Sue, D.W. and Sue, D. (2003) *Counseling the Culturally Diverse.* New York: John Wiley

Sue, D.W., Ivey, A.E. and Pedersen, P.B. (Eds.) *(1990) A Theory of Multicultural Counseling and Therapy.* Pacific Grove, CA, Brooks/Cole.

Suzuki, D. (1997) *The Sacred Balance: Rediscovering our place in nature.* Vancouver: Greystone Books.

Tambini, D. (2001) 'Post-national citizenship. *Ethnic and Racial Studies,* 24, 2, 195-221

Taylor, D. (1996) Citizenship and social power. in D. Taylor (Ed.) *Critical Social Policy: A reader.* London: Sage

Thompson, N. (1997) *Anti-Discriminatory Practice.* Basingstoke: Macmillan.

Thompson, N. (2005) *Understanding Social Work: Preparing for practice.* (2nd ed.) Basingstoke: Palgrave Macmillan

Thompson, N. (1998) *Theory and Practice in Health and Social Care.* Buckingham: Open University Press

Trainer, F. E. (1998) *Saving the Environment: What it will take?* Sydney: University of New South Wales Press.

Tsui, P. and Schultz, G.L. (1985) Failure of rapport: Why psychotherapeutic engagement fails in the treatment of Asian clients, *American Journal of Orthopsychiatry,* 55, 561-569.

Tsui, M.S. (2003) The impact of Chinese culture on social work supervision in Hong Kong. Unpublished paper.

Tsui, M.S. (2004) The supervisory relationship of Chinese social workers in Hong Kong. *The Clinical Supervisor,* 22, 2, 99-120.

Tsui, M.S. (2005) Functions of social work supervision in Hong Kong. International Social Work. 48, 4, 485-493

Tsui, M.S., Ho, W.S. & Lam, C.M. (2005) The use of supervisory authority in Chinese cultural context. *Administration in Social Work,* 29, 4, 51-68

Tu W.M. (1998) Confucius and Confucianism. in W.H. Slote and G.A. DeVos (Eds) *Confucianism and the Family State.* New York: University of New York Press.

United Nations Human Development Programme, (1998) *Human*

Development Report for 1998. New York: Oxford University Press.

United Nations Commission on Sustainable Development, (1999) Texts adopted by CSD-7. (Economic and Social Council, Supplement No. 9). New York: UN Commission on Sustainable Development.

Waterson, J & Morris, K. (2005) Training in 'social' work: exploring issues of involving users in teaching on social work degree programmes.*Social Work Education,* Vol.24, 6, 653-675

Watts, T. (1995) An Introduction to the World of Social Work Education. (quoted in L. Carageta and M. Sanchez (2002) *Globalisation and Global Need.* Sage: London.

Weisner, T.S.(2000) Culture, childhood and progress in Sub-Saharan Africa. in L.E. Harrison and S.P. Huntingdon (Eds.) *Culture Matters. How values shape human progress.* New York: Basic Books

Welfel, E.R. (1998) *Ethics in Counseling and Psychotherapy: Standards, research and emerging issues.* Pacific Grove, CA, Brooks/Cole.

Wenz, P. S. (2001) *Environmental Ethics Today.* New York: Oxford University Press.

Westra, L., & Werhane, P.L. (Eds.) (1998) *The Business of Consumption: Environmental ethics and the global economy.* New York: Rowman & Littlefield.

Wierzbicka, A. (1998) The semantics of illocutionary forces. In A. Kasher (Ed.) *Pragmatics.* Vol. 2. London : Routledge.

Wild, A., Iwami, M. and Meads, G. (2003) Different systems, same issues. *Primary Care Report,* 29th October.

Wohl, J. (1989) Integration of Cultural awareness into psychotherapy. *American Journal of Psychotherapy,* 43, 3, 343-355.

World Bank (1993) *Investing in Health.* Geneva: World Bank.

World Commission on Environment and Development, (1987) *Our Common Future.* New York: Oxford University Press.

World Health Organisation (1988) *Learning Together To Work Together For Health.* Technical Report Series Number 769. Geneva: WHO Publications.

Yip, K.S. (2001) Deep thoughts in the indigenization of Hong Kong social work. *Hong Kong Journal of Social Work,* 35, 1/2, 51-78

Yeates, N. (2005) A global political economy of care. *Social Policy and Society,* Vol. 4, 2, 227-234

Youngelson, H., Neal, A.G., and Fried, J. (2001) Global and local culture in 21st century. *Journal of American and Contemporary Cultures,* 24, 2/3. 31–36

Yuen, S.P. (1998) *Hunyin, Xingbie Yu Xing: Yige dangdai zhongquo nongceen de kao cha.* (2004) [Expanded English translation, 2004: *Marriage, Gender, and Sex in a Contemporary Chinese Village.* New York: M.E. Sharpe]

Yuen, S.P. (2004) *Reconstitution of Social Work Practice in a Hermeneutic Sense.* Singapore: Global Publishing Co.

Zeira, A. and A. Rosen. (2000) Unraveling 'tacit knowledge': what social workers do and why they do it. *Social Service Review,* 74, 1, 103-123.

The contributors

Geoff Mead is Professor of Organisational Research at Warwick University Medical School, Warwick University, England

Andrea Wild is a Senior Research Fellow at Warwick University Medical School, Warwick University, England

Paul McCafferty is the Manager of the Practice Learning Centre at Partnership Care West, Derry, N Ireland

Wilson Muleya Lectures at Kingston University, England

Steve Ambler is a Freelance Trainer based in East Anglia, England

Adrian Black is Programme Manager, Social Work, at City College Norwich, England

Tatanya Tartachnyck is with the Chernihiv law Institute, Ukraine

Dorothy Miller is the Director of the Centre for women, Case Western Reserve University, Cleveland, USA, and Clinical Associate Professor at the Mandel School of Applied Social Sciences

Zita Weber is a Lecturer in Social Work and Policy Studies, and Coordinator of Field Education in the Faculty of Education and Social Work, University of Sydney, Australia

Diana Mak, is Professor Emeritus, and former Head of the Department of Applied Social Studies Hong Kong Polytechnic University, Hong Kong

Graham Ixer, is Policy Advisor at the General Social Care Council, London, England

Elaine Hume is Acting Director of Social Work, Hornsby Ku-ring-gai Health Services, Australia

Fred Besthorn is Associate Professor of social work, College of Social and Behavioral Sciences University of Northern Iowa, USA

Lightning Source UK Ltd.
Milton Keynes UK
UKOW051536241011

180843UK00004B/29/A

9 781861 770516